A Soul Divided

Memoir of a Modern Emigrant

by Maka Kartheiser

A Soul Divided: Memoir of a Modern Emigrant

Published by Maka Kartheiser
Johnsburg, Illinois

Copyright © 2017 by Maka Kartheiser

ISBN-13: 978-1548483289
ISBN-10: 1548483281

Book cover design by Reece Montgomery.
Author photograph by McKenna Montgomery.

From the Editor, to the Reader . . .
    Though I have coached many wonderful people to write their life stories and edited nearly one hundred books so far, rarely have I felt so drawn to an author's heritage, or felt that something was missing from my life by not having been part of it. On the following page, read how Maka describes her native country of Georgia. Believe me, she carries the beautiful spirit of her country within her. I've been blessed to be the recipient of her warm and generous Georgian hospitality, by her openness of heart as she shared her story, and by her quiet strength—and bursts of great humor—as we worked together to bring her autobiography to life.
    Maka invited me to contribute a few thoughts here about my experience working on her story, and working together with her. This is a Georgian publishing custom, one which I find as honoring as I do rewarding. Rarely do editors in the United States experience tangible results from their dedication and long hours, just a twinge of accomplishment and a moment of silence with their computer after clicking "send."
    Maka, you have succeeded once again against difficult odds. May God bless you for having the courage of heart to bring to light more than one time in history that tore your country and your family apart, to share with the reader the genuine experience of the modern immigrant, and to reveal answers you've found to life's universal questions, only through great hardship.
    Thank you for allowing me to accompany you on this part of your journey.
    Now tell me: How does it feel to be holding your book?
                                                  —*Tammy Barley*

All rights reserved. No part of this publication may be reproduced, stored in a retrieval system, or transmitted in any form or by any means without the written permission of the author or publisher.

www.MakaKartheiser.com

Dedication

To my hapless homeland of Georgia, in eastern Europe. Located as a connector of the West and East sides of the globe, this has ever put her between two halves. This is tragic, since from the time she came into existence, she has been unique and so desired by all—emperors and common people alike. This is because Georgia is the culmination of depth of soul, beauty of nature, width of imagination, strength of spirit, kindness of heart, and bravery of character.

To my dad, whose hopefulness was never taken away by a difficult twist of fate.

To my mom, who silently prayed for her children and grandchildren's well-being in a different land, wishing to see that place, but who was never given the chance.

And to my sons, through whose hearts, as a torch, I deliver the love of Georgia.

Contents

Acknowledgements .... *iii*

Chapter One—A Heart Divided 1
Chapter Two—Embassy Story 19
Chapter Three—The Stretching of Wings During Communism 41
Chapter Four—After Collapse of the Soviet Union 59
Chapter Five—Greater Challenges 81
Chapter Six—Braving Unfamiliar Paths 91
Chapter Seven—Foreign Country 109
Chapter Eight—The New Beginning 125
Chapter Nine—Losing Identity 137
Chapter Ten—In It Together 147
Chapter Eleven—"What Is Possible?" 161
Chapter Twelve—Let Your Life Speak 175

About the Author 193

^ Me, during my school years.

Acknowledgements

My deep appreciation goes to . . .

My sons, Levan, Sandro, and Nika, whose endless encouragements and support gave me the confidence to make my story available for readers.

Tom, my husband, who has been challenged many times by our cultural differences, yet has always managed to handle them and has given me the freedom to find myself.

Tammy Barley, my talented editor, who sensed the message I was trying to convey through my story.

Catherine Mosashvili, my dearest friend, who always stands by me, is the first to listen to my thoughts and ideas, and supports me through my journeys.

A brief note to my dear readers . . .

Fellow emigrants—I pray that through my story you will find your own healing and know that you are not alone.

All other readers—I hope *A Soul Divided* will give you a new perspective to see the beauty of living in your homeland and to see that all of us—with our own unique cultures, traditions, and history—are the same, with the same humanitarian feelings of love, caring, the search for our meaning, and the longing to belong!

Far away in the east, over the Atlantic Ocean and across the Black Sea, between Turkey and Russia, there is a small but unique country named Georgia. It was called the Soviet Union before.

I was born there in 1970 and lived under that regime for twenty-one years.

Then I was forced to emigrate from my homeland. Now I live in a new country. I belong to both nations . . . and to neither. Like my fellow emigrants, I am alone among tens of thousands who *do* belong.

Like other emigrants, I am a stranger amid the natural citizens. Another foreign face in a crowd.

I am one of the unseen.

Chapter One
A Heart Divided

Tbilisi, Georgia
May 5, 2004

When life gives you challenges, you have no choice—you have to fight, I tell myself.

"Taxi!" I call.

An old soviet style car rolls to a stop. It is a blocky Jiguli with dark gray paint faded from time and the sun.

I open the back door, squeeze into the small space, and sit on the torn seat without hesitation. The smell of cigarettes, dampness of age, and gasoline hits my nose. It is a common smell in taxi cabs. I do not pay attention. The front seat leans toward me like it has been broken for many years. I ignore this also.

"To Vake, please," I instruct the driver, "and you need to hurry. Please don't procrastinate. Go!"

I don't know if the wide-eyed cab driver senses my urgency, or he is scared of my ordering, or he just entertains the idea that there is going to be a scene like in an action movie, one which might be the highlight of his boring taxi-driving day, but he gets everything in order. He hits the pedal. The engine roars loudly, and the cab speeds forward. Soon the old car is rushing toward the Vake district of Tbilisi.

Anxiousness claws at my heart as the memories of what happened only minutes ago replay in my mind.

※

By eight in the morning, I arrive at the United States consulate, which by this time is so familiar to me. For two of my young sons and myself, I had applied for visas to America. Today will be my interview. Today I will learn whether we will be allowed to go to that country of hope.

The consulate is a two-floor building. It sits in an old, friendly neighborhood of homes that are two or three floors tall. Houses are very close with small yards connecting neighbors. Neighbors often sit in front of their doorways and chat with each other's families.

Fresh laundry floats with a nice breeze, and sun rays shine through white linens. The smell of freshness is in the air. Here and there stand giant, one-hundred-year-old, broad-trunked plane trees. They lay shade over some homes and yards and a few of the only four or five cars parked on the street.

I stand on the asphalt-paved sidewalk in front of the consulate. The sidewalk is not smooth. Over the last years, no one has taken care of it, so in many places the asphalt is chipped away and has holes. Also, the plane tree roots, as they always do, try to find their way above the asphalt, making small hilly bumps. I watch my steps as I walk the thirty or more feet toward the consulate.

At the door, men in uniform stand guard. A crowd of waiting people with papers gives out the feeling that something hopeful is going on here. But other than that, there is not much significant sign that a United States consulate is here.

Outside the consulate, the number of people hoping to go to America, for improving life conditions or education, compared with five years ago, is much less. In 1999, the first time I stood in that line waiting for my turn, three hundred or more people waited. How festively dressed those people came, hoping for their own "visa-getting ceremonial!" In that time America was a brand-new idea, and, as with everything new, exciting expectation glowed in faces. Sparkles of happiness were in people's eyes. Big sparkles.

That waiting went on every day, for years. Each of the times I traveled to America, the number of people applying for visas was a little less. Now perhaps there are only fifty people who stand in line. The sparkle is still here, but it's calmer. They have heard stories from friends and acquaintances about emigrants' wages helping their families to survive. Now their expectations about working as nannies or caregivers, or even just getting visas, are more realistic.

I join them in the line.

"What time is your interview?" someone asks me with curiosity. We are almost each other's competitors here.

"It's at eleven," I answer.

I have a three-hour wait—quite a bit of time to be here.

I don't understand why we come so early if we have an appointed time, but maybe this is a Georgian understanding of an appointment. Or maybe we are so excited for possible opportunities that we can't stay at home. We would rather stay among people with the same interests and talk, and even make jokes with them.

Warmth and the smell of the blooming flowers of May are in the air. The weather definitely is lifting our mood. At this moment everyone sees the future in bright colors, because we are all dreaming of visas to America so we can help our desperate families.

I am thirty-four and a single parent with three sons to provide for. The only work I can find here is 8:00 a.m. to 8:00 p.m., for 4 GEL (Georgian Lari, our currency)—about $1.60 in United States dollars. Not as an hourly wage, but for twelve hours' work. It is not enough to feed anyone.

The door of the consulate opens. Someone's name is called, sending a wave of excitement and also worry through the crowd, because not everyone will be granted a visa to America. A person enters for the first appointment.

Even now, I reflect, nearly fourteen years after the Soviet Union's collapse, people still struggle to find ways to survive.

Growing up, I never thought to live in the United States. I never thought to leave Georgia. Georgia brims with a culture rich in art and literature, and with amazing nature: tall, Swiss-like mountains of the Caucasus, the dramatic Black Sea, and vineyards as beautiful as those of Italy. It is a blessing to call such a place home. Not even soviet rule could take this away.

We tell the following fable about how we came to possess the land we claim to be so beautiful in the world. When God was distributing the land to all the peoples of Earth, the Georgians were feasting, toasting, and doing some serious drinking. As a result, they arrived late and were told by God that all the land had already been distributed.

"What were you doing that was so important you are late for this occasion?" God asked.

"Dear Lord, we are late only because we were lifting our glasses in praise of you."

God was so pleased with the answer that he gave them the part of Earth that was the most beautiful, which he had been reserving for himself.

As a young adult, I became one of the many American emigrants who, during times of complete uncertainty in our native countries, went to foreign lands that gave them possibilities to survive. Emigrants are people tested by life, and their fight for survival is both difficult and painful.

What is the pain for? Homeland-less-ness, parents-less-ness, childhood-friends-less-ness in that cherished, distant foster country. It has given to me so much—house, family, and new friends—yet the ones I have to leave behind cannot be replaced.

Living far away from where my roots are planted, my heart has become divided into two parts. One part belongs to my homeland. The other holds fast to my foster country, the United States of America.

I have endured many sleepless nights with thousands of questions resonating in my mind. Many hours have been lost in guilty feelings about leaving my homeland. "Why did I move out from my country? Why did I leave the place where I had a childhood full of meaningful memories, and parents and friends I could depend on? Why did I come to America? What am I doing here?" And the most confusing, "Where do I belong?"

I live with this pain inside. All emigrants do. This pain will never leave us. Our hearts are always divided.

Person after person walks into the consulate, full of hope. After a time, some come out with quick steps and a serious look on their faces, trying not to connect eyes with anyone. They would love to disappear from waiting people's curiosity. It's impossible, though. Everyone is interested to know where destiny has taken them.

Endless questions start to fly from different areas of the waiting line.

"Have they issued a visa for you?"

"What kind of questions did they ask?"

"What did they tell you?"

These questions stay unanswered, as no one knows why they have not been given the opportunity to go to America.

Others come out with huge smiles on their faces. Their happiness is very quiet, as if they left all their words inside. No one in line asks questions. We know they have gotten visas to the country where dreams are coming true. "Congratulations" fly in the air to the winners. We watch them leave, and then we return to our imaginings that in a few hours we will feel the same happiness.

Finally, it is my turn! I let out a breath of release then enter the doorway.

I am directed to a small room. Inside, five guards stand by security cameras and check everyone who enters.

One of them politely addresses me. "Take out your passport and put your purse here, please."

I hand my passport to him, feeling very happy. I am confident I will be granted the three visas for my sons and myself.

A professional-looking young man flips through my passport and the application form. Then he frowns. "This picture is small! Your photo should be two-by-two inches in size."

My thoughts and heart suddenly traffic-jam together. "What?"

"And whose pictures are these?" he asks. "Are these children trying to apply for visas too?"

"Yes." I feel something unpleasant sink inside of me.

"Where are they?"

"They are at home," I answer with fear.

"Well, everyone who is applying should be here!"

"Should be here? What do you mean?" I am completely confused. I am unable to think.

"Yes, they should be here!" his voice firmly repeats.

"What do you mean? What should I do?" My mind still can't think.

"You need to bring them here."

"How I am going to bring them here? My appointment is at eleven o'clock. It is almost eleven!" In a second everything collapses on me. It took weeks to get this appointment.

All my hopes, all my dreams, all my thoughts scatter. With my eyes I beg someone to tell me what to do.

The young men gather near me. "Well, where are your sons now?" one asks.

Their faces say they want to help. I can feel they are really sincere.

"One is at school. The second one is at home," I mumble.

"Well, what we can tell you is that you can go home and then bring them here. As long you are here before one o'clock, you are good. We know and we will let you in."

They really are trying to help.

Now I know what to do. I have to run.

And I run.

Outside the consulate, people in line call after me. "Hey, ma'am, what's going on?" "Where are you going? Weren't you supposed to have an interview?"

I run, leaving the questions to fade in the sun rays and shadows behind me.

I need to bring my twin sons here . . . and in less than two hours! How am I going to do that?

My mind resumes its processes. A plan comes together in my thoughts. There is no time to lose. Now, actions are needed.

I run to the main street where I will catch a taxi cab.

When life gives you challenges, you have no choice—you have to fight, I tell myself.

"Taxi!" I call.

✺

Now the soviet Jiguli speeds toward the Vake district. I dial my cell phone. My mother answers.

"Mom, you need to bribe Sandro with any possible bribe so he gets dressed. I am coming to pick him up. I need to take the boys to the consulate for an interview, and we have very little time!"

Mom assures me she will. In her voice I hear the same urgency that I feel. We both hang up. With the short call, I have stolen what time I am able.

The first move has been made.

Wanting to go to America, yet wanting to stay in my homeland, I look out the cab window and fill my eyes with Tbilisi.

When I left to go to the consulate, few cars moved in the streets, as the city still lay asleep. Many jobs start around nine or ten each morning, reflecting Europe's laidback lifestyle. Well-rested people have more energy to work, and most don't spend so much money on possessions that they have to work more to pay for it all. They value simplicity of life, but also quality and artistry of effort that beautifies life.

Five-floor condominium buildings in European architectural style appear to be switching each other as the taxi zips past them. Rows of huge plane trees line the way, interspersing my view. Detailed ornamental pieces on buildings, shops with wide gallery windows, sidewalks with wide tiles . . . many times these have been compared with the streets of Paris.

Well-dressed people with business appearance stroll toward destinations. Most women wear dresses and high heels, and men wear dress pants and suit jackets.

Georgian people have an old, rich culture of the arts and love to wear intellectual styles. It is in character to always look presentable, no matter our circumstances.

Gray and dark colors of clothing dominate the streets. Is this a result of Georgia's challenging years? I see seriousness and thoughtful eyes on people's faces. They all have lot on their minds: "What shall I do? How might I improve living?"

These are the worries they have been dealing with since the Soviet Union collapsed.

Well, the university is right here—I just passed by. And there it is—the philharmonic concert hall! Outside it stands the famous bronze statue of *Lady Muse*, an affirmation of Georgia's artistic soul.

The car carries me forward, nearer to three visas to my beloved new foster country.

But my thoughts carry me backward, to my childhood in my treasured homeland of Georgia, to one precious, unforgettable summer when I was twelve.

℘

Summers with my parents and older brother in Kvishkheti, a small village tucked among the high peaks of the Caucasus Mountains in central Georgia, have left an indelible imprint on my young imagination and thinking. It is not merely a village. It is a vacation house for writers and creative people, a place enveloped by beauty and fresh climate.

Many well-known authors and artists, together with their families, spend summer vacations here. They produce new novels, poems, and works of art—inspiring and being inspired.

The first time my parents brought me here, I was three years old. It has been part of my dad's job, as an author with the Georgian Writer's Union, to manage the Kvishkheti library and literary events for vacationers. In this wondrous place, my every July and August is filled with joy and carelessness. Every year the same families and children come and spend time here. It is like being in one big family that we see again every summer. Everyone knows each other, shares similar interests, and is connected.

Originally this huge land and its buildings was the residence of a writer and public person who lived in the late nineteenth century.

A large part of Kvishkheti is surrounded by a green steel-pole fence that is six feet tall. And the gate! It is the same green with a heavy metal door that has a small lock. One has to push down the handle, and you are in! The gate plays a pretty important role. It is a divider between "writers" and "non-writers," as we call vacationers, based on where they stay—either inside the more than five acres of fence line, or outside of it, where vacationers rent houses from the locals. These "non-writers" are equally our dear friends, year after year.

Inside the fence the main building, once the primary residence, now is for us to use. There are about fifty rooms. One room is given in rent to one family, so many families can visit here together. Bathrooms and showers are located in the lower level for shared use.

On the main floor is a huge ballroom with a fireplace. In the center of one wall is a portrait of the writer who lived in this house. The ballroom also holds a large balcony and windows that overlook the grounds.

From the balcony, a breathtaking view opens up. A wide valley with railroad tracks carries a train away to Batumi, a port on the Black Sea. A forest extends as far as eyes can see, and it is mixed—evergreen trees and trees with leaves. The forest covers mountains that form a big bowl around us.

All this picturesque mountain scenery bridges eastern Georgia and western Georgia.

The climate here is freshest, but it also has curative qualities. It cures lung disease, clears lungs, and makes lungs strong again.

The property itself holds tall, century-old Tilia caucasica trees. They form a huge walkway, and green wooden park benches line the walkway's edges, facing each other across the aisle, some with small tables beside them.

These trees are an entertainment for us. They grow green seeds, which themselves hold black seeds inside. We pick the green seeds, open them up, and make black seed necklaces for ourselves. We use sewing thread and needle for this. The black seed is smaller than a sunflower seed, but we very patiently sit, make a hole with the needle, and one after another put seeds on the thread. Sometimes a finished necklace is so long that it reaches to my belly button. We compare and have fun. Who can count how many necklaces we children have made since we began coming here? The names of my girlfriends are Tamara, Eka, Sofio, Nino, Maia. The boys are Gio, Irakli, Sandro, Levan, and David.

The benches have produced cherished memories as well. On every bench a writer sits and writes a poem, thinks about a novel, or worries about characters of a drama piece. Other people sit and draw still life art or paint portraits that museums will one day display, all while we children walk along and watch.

Every afternoon my dad sits on one of the benches with his pen and notebook or with books he has brought along. He is constantly reading or writing. He wears his inseparable black French beret and his glasses, his signature style. His small mustache sits under his nose.

The summer I am twelve, my admiration of his gift stirs me to also become a writer.

Everyone is inspired in this magical, creative place.

This late nineteenth century writer's residence is one of few such residences that survived the hands of the Communist Party. After Communist power spread in the early 1900s, according to their ideology, owners of larger properties or houses across Georgia were seized. Communist philosophy: Take away from the rich and give it to the poor! They evicted the owners of big houses and land, and lodged many poor families on each property.

The destructive path of the Communists has been bloody. Their painful system and practices, which has ruled us for generations, has killed millions of innocent people and tortured the intelligent public into submission.

By odds, however, this particular property in Kvishkheti was not divided between many different families. In favor of intelligentsia, it was transformed into a place where people now spend time creating, where they enrich their imaginations and souls by being closer to nature.

No matter how many forbidden rules we face under Communism, we've had some great life experiences growing up, many of them in Kvishkheti.

∅

In the taxi, holding to the top of the front seat and still about four minutes from home, I reflect that we also experienced many difficult times over the years.

As children, we were left without a choice. We had to become young communists.

From age six to twelve, we were called Octobrist. The name came from the union, which was founded on October 17, 1905. Each of us wore a small medal with a portrait of a six-year-old curly-haired boy named Vladimir, who later was known as Lenin.

Then we grew up a little and became Pioneers. To show our readiness to serve the party, we again wore a small medal with Lenin's teenage face. We also wore red bandanas around our necks, stood straight up, and saluted to the regime.

Every morning a leader of the Pioneers would ask us in a commanding tone, "Young communists, are you ready to serve the Communist Party?"

"We are ready," we had to answer, and no other answer was even considered.

All of us hated this routine, the bandanas, and the whole concept itself. But who would even dare and show their true feelings?

Then as teenagers we turned into Komsomol. The word was an abbreviation of the Russian phrase Kommunisticheskii Soyuz Molodyozhi, which itself stood for All-Union Leninist Young Communist League.

Strict dress codes made all of this worse. Girls wore pleated, brown wool dresses, the same over and over every day. Nothing changed for ten years, only the size of the dress. Guys wore deep blue suits—almost dark gray—and white shirts, all the time. These ugly, boring uniforms induced negative feelings in us. We all looked and felt the same.

The communists definitely blocked individualism in us. The colors of our thoughts were gray and brown, just like the outfits we wore.

Growing up under communism, life itself had colorless colors.

I wore ugly glasses, which was not a surprise. The Soviet Union had no style. Big, heavy frames almost covered my face, but still you were able to see the green eyes, which, over the years, received many compliments. My haircut was short, no particular style or shape. Nothing special.

Memories of my school experience are pretty pale. Over the years I realized how communism did not develop personality qualities in us, nor did it flourish our interests. The soviet system did not encourage individualism as a concept.

The school where I spent all eleven years of my education was prestigious in the city. The lady director, very tough and strict, eventually led the school to success. But we were victims of the soviet system. School reflected the system's requirements. It locked our self-esteem. The "fair" outlined our views—everything was based on fair. That's why no one loved to go to school. Every morning we would go because we had to.

But the soviet educational system had a few good benefits. It provided a wide range of knowledge. We read and studied works of classic writers from all over the world.

The history of the world was taught precisely, which gave us deep knowledge of other countries' highlights.

We learned geography, science, and foreign languages. The Russian language remained as the mandatory language in the entire Soviet Union's school system. Together with the native language, we had to learn Russian from the first grade.

Looking from the positive side, knowing Russian enabled us to read original writings of many great Russian authors.

What we disliked was the history of the Soviet Union, which was based on lies but shown as the greatness of the party.

They tried to engrave this false greatness in every child. Yes, we as children realized all these falsities, but who would disagree? We had to memorize lies and live life with them.

In school, we knew we were taught lies. We didn't like it. And inside of us we, children of the '80s, protested. My generation, unlike my parents' generation, was not that scared. We were quietly rebellious.

Yet I saw firsthand the consequences of censure against free thinking. My brother, Levan, who always had some non-communist ideas, one day faced the pressure of the system.

It was the day his class had a class president's election. Well, the word "election" was just a word, without actual meaning behind it.

Forty-two classmates, boys and girls, all looked very neat on that day, all prepared for the big decision.

At the head of the class, the teacher, Mrs. Lomidze, coldly announced, "Today we are going to choose your class president. Giorgi is nominated to be class president. We will ask you a question, and by raising your hand to agree or disagree, we will decide about Giorgi."

Students' faces didn't show much expression. Students did not think. They just followed whatever would be told.

Satisfied, the teacher started the "voting" process. "Who agrees that Giorgi will be class president for this school year?"

Everyone raised up a hand, without hesitation and without any reaction on their face.

"Is anyone opposed to Giorgi's candidature?" Mrs. Lomidze continued with mandatory responsibility. No one should have disagreed, and she didn't expect that anyone would.

But just as the teacher was going to announce the election's results, my brother raised his hand.

"Levan?" she asked. "What's going on? Why are you raising your hand?"

The teacher did not even connect the idea that someone would reject the nomination of the person she had decided.

"I reject the candidature of Giorgi!" Levan's voice was firm and clear.

"You what? Reject?" Mrs. Lomidze's voice carried irritation and anger that concerned the children.

That day after the break, the principal's assistant approached Levan. "You need to bring your parents tomorrow to school. It is the principal's request!"

My parents were very scared. "Levan, what are you doing to us?"

My parents were summoned to the school in front of the principal and teachers. They were condemned for their son's behavior.

In class Levan's inquisitive mind remained conflicted. He had difficulty with just following what he was told to think or to say without expressing his ideas or opinions.

He wondered, "Why are people not allowed to have a different point of view?"

My mom worried till the death, "Where is he getting all of these 'free' ideas?"

One day I discovered the answer. While I was searching for some item in my parents' closet, I came to a big, heavy sack. Naively I moved it closer and glanced inside. *Magazines!* Big Russian letters read *AMERICA*.

I slid my hand over a glossy cover. The pages were so smooth, so durable. Something mysteriously pulled me closer. My interest was triggered, and I started to flip the pages. Large, colorful pictures of American architecture. Skyscrapers. Jazz musicians.

Articles about American culture, education. Christmas stories and traditions. Christmas songs and musical notes.

It all unfolded in front of my eyes, leaving me in complete astonishment and excitement.

That evening when Dad came home from work, I could not wait until he sat on the couch. Still in hallway, while he was unbuttoning his coat, I asked, "Dad, I found those magazines—*America*! Where are they from?"

"All right, you know about them now," he warned me quietly in the tone that meant I needed to listen, "but make sure you do not talk too much about them."

I agreed.

Dad shared the secret, "Uncle Roman is receiving them at work. Even though soviets refer to the United States as its 'capitalist enemy,' still there is huge interest toward it. Officially these magazines are not permitted for society. They are only reachable by people in higher positions, such as members of the Communist Party. This, itself, is the irony of the system," he commented, "showing that there are gaps between ideology and reality."

Lucky for us to have access to such information! We now knew what real life looked like in America, with its highs and lows. There were articles about many eye-opening elements of life in a free society. Soviets tried to prevent people from seeing colorful and pleasurable life images of the west. But as the saying goes, forbidden fruit tastes better.

Influenced by those magazines, Levan implemented some brave ideas in the family. Once, when he was fourteen, he came up with an idea that left my parents confused and scared. "Mom, Dad, I will be making a turkey dinner, and we will celebrate the

American tradition of Thanksgiving. I will stuff the turkey and cook it with a recipe from the magazine."

After our American Thanksgiving, Levan asked me if I would learn the notes and lyrics of "Holy Night." Paradoxically, lyrics were translated into Russian. My open-minded character quickly supported Levan's ideas. On our brown Belarus piano in the family room, the two of us tried to play and sing the Christmas songs. We celebrated Christmas on December 25 and played Christmas music.

As a growing teenager, I loved American traditions.

And I resented communist rule.

I felt sad that, unfortunately, some countries in this world are less powerful and less fortunate. A big role if they are to succeed and flourish is played by the geographical, political, and environmental conditions and their relationship with neighboring countries.

At the same time, I felt happy that I discovered magazines in Dad and Mom's closet. The photographs. The traditions. The culture of freedom.

∅

The taxi arrives in the Vake neighborhood and stops.

"Wait for me here," I tell the driver. "It should not take too long. I need to bring my sons."

I rapidly squeeze myself out of the car and run toward my building. Thankfully, our condo is on the first floor.

Mom stands by the window, watching for me.

Right away she opens the door. . . .

Chapter Two
Embassy Story

Tbilisi, Georgia
May 5, 2004

"Mom, where is Sandro?"

Mom is quite shorter than she used to be, I realize, feeling by the tightness in my stomach that I will miss her. Is this really happening, that her height is changing with her age? It seems so sad, although I know life flows this way.

I look at Mom again. Her floral gown reaches to her knees. She loves gowns at home, and sleepers, which have the sound of quietness. I remember her always with her red-as-fire hair color, as it is now. I don't even know what her natural color was. The red makes her hazelnut eye color vibrant. She is just that combination—warm as fire, soothing as a floral garden.

Mom has always been very patient. I don't remember her losing her temper, even when my brother and I fought as children. Now, as then, she seems very calm and peaceful as Sandro appears beside her. With a loving voice, she whispers to Sandro, encouraging him to agree and come to the embassy. Sandro does not willingly agree to go to unknown places. Mom combs his golden curly hair and murmurs words as if whispering a prayer.

We are all standing in the front hallway. I patiently wait a few seconds for my mom to gain his agreement.

He is all dressed. Grandma and Grandpa worked hard to bribe him.

Sandro did not go to school today. A few days ago, we rushed him to the emergency room. He crashed into an iron pipe in the street while playing roughly and cut his eyebrow. Doctors put in nine stitches. Half of his eyebrow is covered with green medicine.

Sandro seems more relaxed today. Either yesterday's accident or today's bribery put him in a different mood than usual. He is seven years old and will be eight in about one month. But he's pretty tall and big for his age. That confuses people, who treat him as older, but soon Sandro's behavior helps everyone realize that he is younger.

"Sandro, my dear, let's go,"—suddenly I am switching my voice to very sweet and entertaining—"I will take you to have an ice cream! I will buy you Coke!"

I'll do everything! I am promising everything. Now it only matters that he agrees to come with me.

"Are you really?" He is suspicious. I almost never let them have Coca-Cola.

"Yes, my dear. Let's go!" I grab him by hand, and we both run with some excitement out the doorway.

We jog to the taxi, squeeze inside, and I say, "Paliashvili 159, please!"

Soon the taxi pulls up in front of the school where Sandro and Nika attend second grade.

"Please wait for us here," I order the taxi driver. "I need to get my other son from the class. It should not take long."

By now the driver is patiently understanding.

We run again, Sandro keeping up with me and smiling. I think Sandro likes this excitement. He must also think this is some action movie scene.

We run up to the third floor because there is no elevator. When we top the stairs, I pause to catch my breath. But who cares if I am out of breath? Now there is only one aim—the embassy!

I pull Sandro down the hall to the correct door. "Nika's class is here," I say needlessly, as if talking will speed up time and get us there faster. After a modest knock on the door, I open it. "Excuse me. I have to take Nika out—it is an emergency!"

The teacher nods. Nika grabs his books, stuffs them into his backpack, and comes.

In the hallway he asks, "What's going on, Mommy?"

Already I start toward the stairs. One boy is on each side of me. "Nika, we have no time for questions. We have to run. A taxi is waiting for us."

We run. Nika and Sandro are enlivened by my energy. The boys definitely think this is an action movie.

Outside, all three of us crowd into the narrow backseat. "Rustaveli Avenue, please!" As the car accelerates forward, I smile sunbeams down at my twin sons. "Boys, now we will go to take *pictures*—is that not fun?" I am pretending that all is funny and exciting. I need to gain their trust.

"Okay, Mom!" The boys are very enthusiastic now. They don't care what we do.

"Driver, please stop here!"

Apparently, he heard "take pictures." The car is halting in front of the photo shop on the main street of Tbilisi.

I open the door. "Driver, we will be—"

"Right back." The driver rests an elbow on the rolled-down window and watches us jump from the cab. As we hurry in, he turns the car on a dead-end street and waits.

Inside the shop I frantically say, "Pictures, please!" It seems everyone feels the urgency. Passports photos are taken, and then we are back in the taxi. "The embassy, please!"

The taxi driver definitely is having a thrilling morning.

Or maybe he feels we have a serious issue.

Or maybe he feels I will pay him nice.

One way or another, he is excellent. We are back to the embassy at noon. I pay him extra, and he drives off, perhaps while taking a breath of relief.

We run to the consulate. The people in line and security guards greet us like we are old acquaintances. The boys are happy. Sandro's eyebrow, painted green, makes everyone cheerful.

"Oh, you are here! How cute are your boys!" Many people give all kinds of compliments.

The joy in my heart fizzes up and over the top.

Security guards check our documents once again. Everything seems satisfying. We pass through security under a watchful camera then enter a room.

The room.

There are lots of chairs placed in a few rows. Like all the other Georgians here, the boys and I sit quietly. Who knows how many emotions and thoughts these people's minds are going through? Nervously everyone waits for their name to be called, and then, one by one, we will approach the small window.

On the other side of it sits the consul, defining our destiny for the next months of our lives.

When the boys and I are called up, the consul asks us a lot of questions. I am giving my answers. He seems okay with them.

And we are given three visas.

Outside, everyone congratulates us! I do not think it often happens at the consulate that a young mother and two of her children receive visas!

Leaving our new acquaintances behind, I take Sandro and Nika for the promised bribes. I buy them ice cream and Coca-Colas. I even buy an extra Coke for Levan, their older brother, who is ten years old and will stay in Georgia this time.

We enjoy our ice creams, then we jump into a trolley bus and start back to our condo. In about two months, we will be packing our suitcases! How exciting!

With Cokes still in our hands, we arrive home. We ring the bell ceremonially before stepping inside.

"We are home!"

Mom and Levan run to meet us and hear our news.

"We are going to America!" I declare, excited, joyful, and smiling just as big as Sandro and Nika are.

But the joy freezes inside me when I see instant change on Levan's face.

Without words, he leaves the hallway and goes into the living room.

I know something is happening in his small, caring, and loving heart. I stop my joy and quietly follow.

I sit beside him on the couch. "Levaniko, what's going on, my dear? You are sad, but you know we will come back very soon, right? It is just six months, then we be home, like the time you and I went to America."

A sob breaks out from his little chest. All at once he is crying profusely. Tears run down his cheeks.

I freeze motionless. Words stick in my throat.

After a time, the telephone rings. My brother in Chicago has also been waiting to hear the news.

"Hello, Maka. So did you get your visas?"

"Everything is good," I tell my brother, Levan, whom my son is named for. "We have visas. But Levaniko is crying. He now realizes, all the way, that we are truly going and won't be with him for some time."

"He is crying?" Uncle Levan is very sad to hear about his nephew. "Maka, why did you even think about leaving him? Why didn't you plan to bring him with you?"

"What?" Suddenly everything collapses on me. "What are you talking about, Levan? Bring him with me? I thought you only have room for three of us. Why did you not tell me before?"

Momentarily, in my head, I plan to apply for a visa for Levaniko.

Two days later, I return to the consulate.

The same security guards are on duty. They recognize me right away and are very attentive. "Ma'am, did you forget something?" one of them asks politely.

"No," I say calmly, "I am here to find out if I could apply for a visa for my third son."

"A third son?" All eyes turn toward me in astonishment. "Are you out of your mind?" a guard blurts out. "They just let you to take two sons to America, and after two days you dare to come back and ask permission for your third son?"

They cannot hide their surprise that I have even dared to think of asking. To get a visa is not easy. People shake and tremble to ask for only one visa.

"My son cried that he would not see us for six months. So I would love to try to get a visa for him as well. If all our visas are rejected because of it, I'll know it was not meant to be." I am sure in my decision.

It appears the guards have never seen anyone with this brave idea about risking three visas in order to ask for a fourth.

Later, when I return home, I have an interview date about a possible visa for Levan!

A few days later, I speak again to the consul. The consul, without any hesitation, grants Levan a visa to travel with us to the United States.

Soon, all four of us bounce about in excited preparations for our upcoming travel.

༄

Our flight will depart at dawn. As we ready ourselves the night before to leave the condo, we fully realize we will be gone six months—far away from home, family, and everything familiar to us.

Mixed feelings float in the air: excitement, sadness, anxiety, rush, striving toward the light.

And one thing is out of order. Sandro is in bed with a high fever of 102. He's had the fever four days already, but with no other symptoms.

"Mom, what's wrong with this child?" I catch Mom while she prepares supper for the family. I am confused, and when I am confused, usually I turn to my mom. She knows everything better than I do. Yes, there were times I thought I knew everything and would not want to listen to her advice, but with motherhood and age I have gained more wisdom.

"I think he is struggling with emotions, Maka." Her mother's instincts give her confidence to say this.

Sandro doesn't fully understand what the upcoming trip is promising or offering him and his brothers. But he definitely knows he will miss playing with friends, running in the yard, summer vacations in Kvishkheti's adventurous mountains, his grandparents' love and care, Grandpa's bedtime stories, and Grandma's lullabies. This is his homeland. This is his home. And now he fears things are going to change.

He is helpless. His brothers too. Mother made a decision, and the small boys have to follow.

The next morning, I wake him. "Sandro, my dear"—my soft, loving, and caring voice must convince this little boy—"everything will be okay, you know, right? We will see so many exciting things. Uncle Levan is waiting for you. He will take us to some wonderful places, like zoos and parks. Please get up. Let's get dressed. There is much good that is awaiting us."

I am sad that I will take the boys away from loving grandparents, but we must go to another country for now.

We insist, his brothers begging too, so Sandro gets up from the bed. He seems very weak and pale. I help him to dress, pretending that all is good, that there is no such thing as a child with a fever. We cannot miss the airplane. We can't lose four tickets. There is no way!

The boys behave nicely as we proceed to the airport, through security checking, and into the airplane. Maybe the excitement of a strange place is quite a shocking experience for these small boys' imaginations?!

꙰

The first flight, from Tbilisi to Athens, takes about three hours. The boys fall asleep after all that precious excitement, and I am relieved. I feel quite sleepy myself.

Next we change planes for our trip from Athens to Chicago. This flight will take eleven hours.

We find our seats in a huge Boeing. There are quite a few small children on board. Flight attendants are very attentive and caring toward small passengers.

A family, an American father and a Greek mother with three young children, sits right next to us. All six of our children play well together hour after hour, and for me it makes time go a little faster.

My main concern is Sandro. But he seems all right. He plays with the children and does not seem emotional or sad.

As we fly over Europe away from home, my thoughts travel back to Georgia, to when I was about my children's age. I had many concerns at that age as well. One of the biggest wasn't fear of losing myself. It was trying to discover who I was while under oppressive soviet rule.

∅

"Dad?" I sit and look up at my father. "Do we belong to Europe or Asia?" It has often been a historical argument whether we belong to Asia or Europe.

At his desk, Dad leans back and assembles his thoughts. His explanation on every subject is detailed and includes many facts. As a writer, this is his way. "It has been a tough dispute, my dear," Dad begins, and his gaze rests on me. "After long research by historians, linguists, archeologists, and geographers, after they considered many facts about Georgian cultural identity, our Orthodox Christian religion, our nation's borders, social connections, traditions, and educational values throughout the centuries—especially from the nineteenth century—" he leans toward me, pleased at my interest in our homeland, "they came to the conclusion that Georgia has been influenced by European architects, writers, artists, education, and fashion. Therefore, Georgia is considered part of Europe."

In our communist-controlled schools, learning the history of Georgia as part of the Soviet Union is mandatory, but because of my dad's great knowledge, my brother and I can be exposed to the truthful side of it. I am nearly a teenager, and ready to understand more of what my father knows.

"Dad, when and how did Georgia really become under soviet ruling?"

About matters which my brother and I can learn for ourselves with a little help, Dad does not just tell us the answers. "My dear, go bring the encyclopedia, ninth book, and let's read together."

The eleven books of the big Soviet Encyclopedia are among those books which every Georgian owns. There are a few series of books among that list, *Georgian Prose*, *Georgian Poetry; The Knight in the Tiger's Skin*, and a few more.

I get up heavily. I don't like when my dad does not give us ready answers. But he sometimes reminds me that it is wise to teach children to find their own answers, and I know how much education and effort my parents and grandma put into my brother's and my right learning.

I slide the glass which covers the bookshelves so the books do not get dusty. One whole shelf is filled with black, huge books, containing valuable information. I find the one Dad indicated, then squeeze it out since they are so tight fitted here. My hand opens the cover and turns pages while I walk back to my dad's desk, trying to find the right page.

When I locate the listing for Georgia, I sit with him. Together we find the answers.

The Russian Empire's drive to expand its power over nearby territories came long before the wretched birth of communism. According to the Treaty of Georgievsk, written at the end of the eighteenth century between the Russian Empire and the East Georgian Kingdom, Russia took responsibility to protect Georgia from the invasive neighboring Muslim countries. The results were disappointing, as Russia failed to uphold its obligations.

Over time the Georgian Kingdom was transformed to a province and annexed by the dominant Russian Realm.

When the Marxist Social Democratic Labor Party won with a majority of votes in Russia, Bolsheviks, the name which comes from *bol'shinstvo*, meaning *majority*, became the new leaders. They rose to power in Russia during the October Revolution in 1917.

Founded by Vladimir Lenin and eventually led by Joseph Stalin, Bolsheviks were the working class of Russia. The Bolsheviks ultimately became the Communist Party in the Soviet Union.

After the Russian Revolution in 1917, some politically powerful Georgians went against the soviets, resulting in a brief period of independence. Three years later, in 1921, the Soviet Red Army annexed it once again and has ruled over it since.

Representatives were placed in every soviet republic, including Georgia, and the agents would do anything to prove their loyalty to the party.

The beginning of the twentieth century was a difficult time for small nations that had fallen under the communist's despotic regime. This was a period full of the bloodshed of innocent people. Perhaps every family was affected by repressions of soviet injustice.

"Georgia borders Russia," Dad points out. He rubs his eyes as if to ease pain there. "Simply because of geographical location, Georgia is at the heart of hot and conflicting political events."

I watch his expression, and wonder about *him*, the grandparent I never knew.

"Dad," I say softly, "tell me about your father."

He becomes still.

Before now I have heard only pieces of what happened. "What became of him?"

It is hard for my dad to go back in memories. And with communist agents everywhere, it is difficult to feel safe to speak.

He says, "I was a nine-year-old boy." Then he is quiet again.

I can see in his face that his memories burn as terrible as fire, and by his silence I know the words are bitter as ash.

"It was 1937," he says. "This was the bloodiest year of executions. Neighbors and other people were arrested and killed if they were suspected of possibly opposing the communist regime. A man could be killed if someone in power simply became jealous of his accomplishments, knowledge, or because he had served as an officer in the king's army," he explains. "The most simple and worthless motives for destroying people's lives could have been owning a large property, having a good job, or having a beautiful wife if a communist leader had an interest in her."

The lines of his face seem to become heavier, as if weights are pulling on them. The rims of his eyes darken with grief. "In most cases, the reasons for these arrests, just like in my father's case, were never known to us.

"In the middle of one night, in autumn, disguised strangers knocked on our door. My father, Kasiane, opened it. 'You need to come with us!' the men told him, and they grabbed him and took him away. That was all."

My imaginings labor to piece together what "that was all" means.

Dad says, "They executed him."

My heart grows as heavy as Dad's expression.

"Soon after my father's death, my mother, Margaret—she was a Russian language teacher at a local school then—she was also arrested and taken away from us. Her only blame was failure to reprove my father to the government. For that sin, she was exiled to Siberia and forced to stay there for eight years, away from her children and her homeland.

"Siberia is the coldest part of Russia," he reminds me. "The freezing climate physically impaired or destroyed many prisoners. The average winter temperature in Siberia could be -5 to -25 Celsius, 23 to -13 Fahrenheit. Such a winter was desperately challenging, especially for people from Georgia, who are used to a warmer, more tropical climate.

"My mother was one of the imprisoned women who were called 'the wives of the people's enemies.' Like all the women there, my mother had no fault, other than being wife of her executed husband."

I have no words to say to Dad. What can anyone say?

The clock on the wall ticks long moments away, but Dad does not notice. He has more to share with me.

"When my dad was executed and my mother taken to Siberia, my two older brothers, Gedevan and Avtandil, were students at the university here in Tbilisi. I went to live with our uncle and aunt's family in a small village in the west region of Georgia. Later, Gedevan became captain of a ship and took ship through the Black Sea to the wide oceans. Avtandil, professor of linguistics at the university, was continuing his already successful research about languages and their structures.

"But two years after our father was killed and our mother exiled, World War II began. The Soviet Union called everyone of age to fight against Germany. Gedevan and Avtandil were among the first to be called to fight for 'the country.'

"Sadly, both of my brothers were soon killed in the war. Our mother would never see them again."

The clock slowly ticks moments by.

Dad says, "The irony of this was the fact that the Soviet Union had killed and damaged both of our parents, but now my brothers had to fight for that country. After they were gone, I stayed on with my uncle and aunt. They took care of me until I was nineteen."

Dad's father was taken away in the night, I realize, when Dad was only about nine years old.

He taps the Soviet Encyclopedia, which reveals none of the history he has witnessed, and he speaks even more softly. "The executions lasted until after Stalin's death, in the 1950s, though other types of devastations have continued, just like throughout all the decades of soviet rule. Many of those who survive physically are nearly destroyed by mental torture. People's thoughts and conversations are controlled, as you have seen from your years growing up, Maka, and the freedom of speech is beyond mentionable."

If someone were standing more than a few steps away from Dad and me, they would not be able to hear his words, but I am sure I will not forget them.

From reading the *America* magazines and learning what freedom must be like, I know that the people of Georgia and of other nations under soviet control are deprived of their personal choices. The Communist Party is the leading and ruling party. They define the thinking and mentality of everyone in society. No one is permitted to think what the communists do not tell them to think.

To be certain this is so, their agents are secretly everywhere.

"If you want to get successful, you need to be a member of the party." When I was a child, one day these words slipped out from Mom's lips. Everyone knew that was true. Just no one would dare to say it out loud and complain. I recall the memory for Dad now, in a trembling voice just above a whisper.

Dad nods that he agrees with Mom's words. "Adults still have a choice to become members of the party or not. Although if not, you are not given leading positions at work. But many choose not to. I choose not to. I cannot swear loyalty to the party that destroyed my family, my childhood. That would mean I forgive them the injustice, not only to my family but to millions of others."

I understand. As children, we've not had a choice. We've had to become young communists—Octobrist, then Pioneers, then Komsomols. Every morning we have to solute a communist leader and promise we are ready to serve the party.

The schools we attend do not allow us to choose. Nor do they develop personality values. We are not encouraged to have a dream.

My brother, Levan, however, often pushes the boundaries of free thinking. First it was a disagreement with his teacher over who the class president would be. The next time had been a hunger strike, a form of protest manifested in western capitalistic countries.

Soviet TV news channels showed these protests as terrible and negative aspects of a capitalistic society, not as a way to express free thinking. Levan instead saw it as freedom of expression.

"Maka, are you going to support me?" Levan asked me.

"What are you going to do?" I said quietly, not all the way sure we were doing something appropriate.

"We pretend that I am on hunger strike." Levan showed me a big poster which said *The seventh day of fasting.*

I smiled. I knew he was doing this to get attention. Around six at night, our mom and dad came home from work.

We greeted them with the poster.

"What are you guys doing?" My dad's strict voice seemed a little shaky.

"We are on hunger strike!" Levan's voice sounded firm.

"Why?"

"Because you don't let me hear the Voice of America radio program. It's full of interesting information."

In the '70s and '80s, the devices which would catch long waves on the radio weren't accessible, so my dad purchased one on the black market. While we were sleeping, Levan sneaked to listen to the Voice of America radio broadcast. That channel broadened his perspectives: new ideas, free thinking, political and economic news, and much eye-opening information.

Jazz and blues music poured from the radio receiver like a feeding stream. Levan became a fan of Louis Armstrong, Bing Crosby, Ella Fitzgerald, and Duke Ellington.

That device also helped him to learn the English language. Listening to news, songs, and radio hosts' speech became a natural teacher for him.

My parents gave up.

Once Levan acted as a homeless person living in the streets.

"Maka, we will use that empty TV box, as an imitation of my living space. Are you going to help me?"

He would always include me in his ideas, as he knew I would support him.

My parents were scared to death of Levan's dissident ideas, and kept trying to talk him into being "normal." But he longed to think freely, to have new experiences. He dreamed to be able to travel and see other countries to expand our horizons.

"Why can't people buy airplane tickets and travel to other countries if they would like to?" he would ask.

My heartbroken parents begged him not to speak these ideas to anyone except them.

⌘

As freedom of thoughts and opinions are forbidden under the communist dictatorship, so is God and church, in schools and in general. No kind of expression of religion is allowed to manifest, not even if it is hidden and unseen. Such things are aggressively removed, as is everything that might lead children to feel like individuals or think for ourselves.

At the age of sixteen, I am secretly baptized. My godmother, Nargiza, gives me a gold cross necklace as a gift. I wear the necklace, but it is completely concealed underneath my boring brown school uniform.

It is 1986.

On a Monday morning, I wake up at my usual time, seven forty-five. I put on the same dress I always have to wear, and get ready for school. Then I pick up my heavy school bag with its long strap. The bag is as plain and dreadful looking as my gloomy uniform. Nothing in the Soviet Union has any sparkle of light within. My room, my home have little color. Even outside, the town is like an extinguished candle.

The bag is so heavy I have to hold up the shoulder that bears the strap and lean over the opposite way to carry it. If someone were to photograph students going to schools, the picture would have a pattern—identical bags and leaning children.

I open the front door and descend three flights of stairs.

"Good morning, Aunt Lida." Like every morning, I politely greet my first-floor neighbor, who sits every single morning by her window and watches each person pass by right or left.

Sometimes we children ask each other, "Is she a spy? Does someone pay her to sit there permanently and watch people? Does not she have something to do around the house?" Partly we joke. Partly we wonder.

We will never know for sure, but it is common to have one agent per each house, or classroom, or workplace. Someone is always listening to our spoken thoughts, counting our steps.

Streets are not so busy this time of day. Other than walking, trolleybuses and buses are the main transportation. Cars are a luxury. Not many people can afford to drive them.

I take my usual route to school. It is a fifteen-minute walk.

I turn left and enter the school grounds through the metal gate. The stream of children who approach the entrance stop and gather outside the door. I see representatives of the school board move roughly among the students nearest to them.

The crowd of students is unusually quiet.

"What's going on?" I ask the girl next to me.

"I think they are checking everyone for unnecessary jewelry, earrings, scarves, or anything else illegal we might be wearing."

The girl seems worried. Everyone else is worried also. We do not know what we are about to get.

As I approach, I see them check each child's neck for any possible forbidden symbols.

Then the principal stops in front of me. "Open the buttons. Let us see your neck!" Her cold voice cuts the air.

My fingers start to shake as I open my neck buttons.

The fine golden chain surrounds my neck.

"What is hanging on this chain?" Her fierce, cold voice is gauged to crush my heart.

My lips tremble. I cannot hear my own voice when I form the words, *A small cross.*

"What is this!" Her angry voice is like fire. "How do you *dare* to wear a cross at school? Take it off!"

"W-what?" My knees are about to buckle.

"Take it off!" She orders me in that heartless voice.

I try to take off my precious piece.

The principal is too anxious to wait. She tears it from my neck, scoring my skin.

I feel pain not only on my body but inside my heart.

"Bring your parents tomorrow to school!" I hear her strict, cold voice as she gives my chain to another teacher who holds a box full of extracted necklaces.

As children, each of us has a need to discover who we are, and longs to express the person inside. Under soviet rule, that is not possible. It is forbidden.

But like my brother Levan, I want to discover my self. More and more, I want to know who Maka truly is, when no one tells her what she can and cannot say, or what she can and cannot wear.

※

No matter how many forbidden rules we have faced, we've also had great life experiences growing up.

Reading and education are important values, thanks to my parents, as well they are cultural values. My dad's work itself is a continual inspiration. The Georgian Writers' Union, the building with an extraordinary history, is part of my childhood too.

"Guys, get ready. Tomorrow we will go to my workplace. We will take lunch, snacks, and spend all of Sunday in its beautiful garden. We will read books. Also you will help me to organize books alphabetically, and we will use the day sufficiently."

On many weekends my dad makes our days into celebrations as we visit this amazing building. I feel writing and books pull at hidden places inside of me.

The next morning I get up early, excited for upcoming day trip. Dad's workplace is right in the center of Tbilisi, but the building will relocate us into a variety of creative worlds.

I hold my dad's hand and almost fly from the happiness. Our fifteen-minute bus ride is festive too, as I think about the interesting day awaiting me.

On the last station, Lenin Square, the bus driver announces, "The last stop! Everyone should get out here!"

We do. Right here is the "Universal" store. It is four floors, where you can buy mostly everything. Well, whatever is available to us.

We walk far beneath the large, high statue of Lenin that holds his right hand over us. We did not care for the statue, but we have to pass this place often.

We walk down Main Street. Then gradually the street curves right, and a cobblestone street appears. After a minute, we turn onto small, quiet Machabeli Street in the center of Tbilisi. The old, architecturally beautiful building is only steps away.

Built in 1905, the building has functioned as headquarters of the Georgian Writers' Union since 1921. It's had a big history itself. The giant, sand-colored edifice was the project of a German architect who designed curled front moldings, ornamental shells over giant, arched windows, and wavelike window moldings that flow from the centers of shining glass panes.

Inside, our footsteps echo along wide hallways and in huge rooms with tall ceilings. The rooms are decorated with statues of famous Georgian writers, portraits of famous people, carved antique desks that serve many talents, a grand piano, and books, books, and more books, all on mahogany shelves. These are classics of Georgian authors and those of foreign writers.

I feel the presence of great, talented spirits here.

For this day, I can be whoever I want to be: a princess locked in a castle waiting for the prince on a white horse, or a pirate. I can journey to Treasure Island, or travel around the world.

For now, in my imagination, there is no soviet oppression of Georgia.

Chapter Three
The Stretching of Wings
During Communism

Tbilisi, Georgia
1987

A year has passed. I have become a student at Tbilisi State University, TSU, which was founded in 1918. Located in the heart of the city, TSU is my temple of knowledge and pride. This morning I walk up the lane, thinking it is an amazing experience to spend the most valuable years of youth in the building where many famous Georgians studied and flourished in their talents—intellectual writers, historians, physicists, mathematicians, linguists, and scientists.

Dad attended this university too. He graduated it on a Silver Medal, which means excellent grades. His two older brothers, Gedevan and Avtandil, also studied here, before they were forced to fight in World War II for the Soviet Union.

Because of so many connections to this university, I am happy to study here.

So far, my student life at TSU has been unforgettable. The university garden, with its statues of TSU's founders, surrounds the main building. The garden itself serves as a gate to a future full of possibilities. Each morning starts here with ritual greetings before the day's educational journey starts. Students, friends, and even lectors spend time here meeting and sharing news with each other.

"Hey, Nino, how are you?" I call. "Hi girls!"

"Maka, good to see you."

"Good morning, Professor Lominadze!"

The garden is the place where we fill our souls with sun and friendship. In the park, centenarian trees give shade and comfort. Their strength is transmitted.

Benches are always full of students. Poets read poems to their peers. Others talk together, and someone sings while playing a guitar.

This place is full of life itself. It is where we fortify respect, appreciation of one another, and friendships.

"Buy the flowers for your loved ones. Buy the flowers, please." The voice of an old man with a wrinkled face is encouraging love. Wild spring flowers tied in small bouquets are for sale.

"These flowers are for you!" All of a sudden, my friend Giorgi hands me a bouquet. There is no special reason necessary for a boy to give flowers to a girl. Just a casual friendship is reason enough to make someone else feel amazing.

"Oh, how wonderful!" I bring the bouquet to my nose. The wild smell of mountain fresh air and untouchable beauty pour inside of me. With a smile, I continue on my way, still enjoying the smell of the flowers.

And then the big white building of European architecture style arises on the hill, standing strong. Soon I open a huge wooden door that is almost as tall as two people, and enter.

Clean white painted walls border solid, white marble floors. I take a deep breath, filling my lungs with the air of knowledge, and then walk straight to the marble stairs. They lead me up to the second floor where the auditoriums are.

Similar tall, strong wooden doors open to auditoriums with high ceilings. The open space gives the feeling of freedom, promising a sky of possibilities.

Mr. Parulava, a middle-aged professor, is known as a strict lecturer. About one hundred twenty students search for their seats. I find my spot, and the bell rings!

Silence is king now.

In these auditions, I learn the depth of linguistics, mysteries of mythology, secrets of teaching, and treasured writing skills. But most of all, humanity, love, and friendship.

Between classes, as we hurry up or down sunlit stairways in the eighty-year-old building, our footsteps and happy laughter echo. My best friend, Tako, is a talented artist and takes many art classes. I want so much to draw too, and I have the chance to take art classes.

But sadly, I do not pursue this. I cannot find the courage. Fear of trying something new, and fear of making bold decisions, is part of the soviet ideological mentality. Our parents' suppressed thinking does not let our young generation think freely and openly. Our parents' fears are deeply rooted in the repressions and punishments of the Stalin Era.

Fear limits thinking. Fear prevents thought about new possibilities.

The fear of anything new—new ideas, technological development, political changes, or even differing opinions under soviet rule—overwhelmingly affects people's mentality and limits their ability to advance.

Fear holds me back many times. At the university, I never explore the artist inside of me.

I have many times of happiness at the university while learning and stretching my wings, but fear and limitations hold me back from discovering who I am and how I might contribute to the world.

✒

My brother, Levan, also attends the university. He studies at the TSU Linguistics Department with an English language major. Like many boys his age, he does not communicate much about his plans, including his educational events, with the family.

One evening during dinner with our parents, grandma, and aunt, Levan has something unexpected to share.

"Hey, everybody, I have great news! I am going to study in America at a big university for one whole school year!" Levan declares in a voice full of unknowns but also with alluring prospects of a potentially bright future.

Everyone except for Levan is in shock.

"What are you talking about?" The family questions Levan. I can feel the fear in their voices. Everyone seems confused. They look at each other with scared eyes, trying to see each other's reaction.

For my parents, grandma, and aunt, talking—even dreaming—about America is unimaginable, unthinkable. Levan's "news" sounds not only unrealistic but also scary. They remember Levan's innovative ideas from previous years. They remember facing school board consequences because of those ideas.

None of us knows what to feel, to be happy or to be scared.

In the days that follow Levan's announcement, puzzle pieces slowly start to fall into place. More information becomes available, and our confusion gradually disappears.

We learn that American professors and educational groups tested students for their knowledge of the English language, with the idea to send the best ones to study abroad. Levan won the contest.

Slowly, everyone becomes used to the possibility of Levan's upcoming educational plans.

This is the time for exchanging educational experiences. The cold war climate is finally warming up.

∽

Tbilisi, Georgia
April 9, 1989

I am nineteen years old and a student in my second year at the TSU. Life is full of hopes, future exciting plans, and dreams for us students, the young people of Georgia. The Soviet Union's political policy of limiting free-thinking has slowly started to loosen its controlling ties on society. In the air are new, previously unknown breezes of possible freedom. Political relationships are easing between Cold War countries, Russia and the United States of America. We see hope on the horizon.

Anti-soviet movements started slowly in 1988 and have gained popularity among the naturally free-thinking Georgians. But while freedom became our goal, Georgia's west coast by Black Sea became disputed region. Abkhazians, the Caucasian ethnic group living in Abkhazia, the land which belongs to Georgia, also started having their own ideas about independency from Georgia, ideas which were influenced and escalated by Russia. Abkhazians sought to become part of Russia, but little did they know they would soon be used for Russia's dictatorship goals and eventually neglected.

The subject became very touchy, since historically the large territory belonged to Georgia and we did not want to see it put itself back under the Russian boot, especially because for the first time in seventy years we are nearly out from beneath it. The issue caused protests among Georgians, and the students of the universities were the most disturbed by it. More and more people joined anti-soviet groups to protest.

The protesting reached its peak on April 4, when tens of thousands of Georgians gathered in front of the Parliament Building. Each day after, the number of protesters grew and grew.

The morning of April 8, as on the previous days, I am in a fellow student's peaceful protest group at the university. We are young, and the sun is shining on the stairs of the main building of the university, where all of us, excited with togetherness and with possible freedom, laugh, sing, and are full of joy.

As I would learn later, we did not fully understand the whole weight that politics held.

On this morning, the leader gains our attention and announces, "Everyone, let's get going! We are heading to Rustaveli Avenue."

"Tako, Kethie," I say to my best friends, feeling as if instincts are trying to warn me of danger, "Let's stay together, girls."

Huge crowds head along Melikishvili Avenue. It is hard to move easily, as hundreds, maybe thousands, of us are all squeezed so close. When we reach the Parliament Building area, we see speakers talking through *rupori* (megaphones) with strong statements to defend freedom.

Hours pass, and after hearing many speakers, we get tired. I decide to leave the meeting and go home, still feeling that something bad will happen. It is close to six o'clock in the evening.

We now live with my maternal grandma and my mom's unmarried sister, Aunt Thea, because Grandma broke her leg and needs care. When I arrive back home, only Grandma is there. "Grandma, where are Levan, Dad, and Mom?"

"Levan wouldn't change his mind, and your parents went with him to the protest to make sure things are okay."

I hear worry in Grandma's voice.

☙

Near the Parliament Building, my dad and mom stay near Levan. "Rezo," my mom says close to my father's ear, "there are so many protestors."

"Zaira," he answers, "I don't really like the tension of this event anymore. The experience of protests during the Stalin era is alerting me."

Dad notices that everyone is being directed to the opposite side of the Parliament Building, by the movie Theater Rustaveli, where university students are grouped together. A door of the theater stands open, and an elderly lady with a small broom is sweeping the cigarette butts and dust.

The number of protesters is growing.

"Levan, Zaira, let's stay near the street corner. In case something happens, we can leave the area."

Thankfully, Levan stays close.

Rezo is worrying. Suddenly he notices this point of escape is blocked by a strange looking pickup truck, which clearly has no reason to be in downtown, especially now, during the meeting. This is a red flag. Something is happening.

"We need to stay together!" Rezo warns over and over. "I don't like the way things are developing here."

A speaker talks loudly through a *rupori*. Then he announces, "Now our Patriarch will have a word!"

The crowed quiets. The Patriarch of the Georgian Orthodox Church steps to the top of the stairs. An attentive eye might notice the tension in his otherwise peaceful appearance, but no one has time now for this kind of surveilllance.

The crowd becomes motionless and is all ears. Ilia II starts speaking slowly, the way he usually speaks, in his deep voice.

Everyone respects him and awaits his words, but they all want to hear words of encouragement for going forward. Instead they hear the caring words of a parent who fears danger and warns his children. "My dear brothers and sisters, daughters and sons. Georgia stands on a very dangerous path. Go home, everyone, go home. . . ."

But when does the child listen to the parent? When would the inexperienced take the advice of the experienced? When would the new generation take the mistakes of previous generation into consideration, and learn from them to make their path easier?

Or maybe the steps are uninheritable? Maybe the tragedy is needed for them to learn?

Unhappy, they do not listen to what they need to hear. They start to move about, resuming the protest. They see but do not fully realize why huge green tanks are moving slowly closer to crowd. Instead, Georgian spirits start to sing, naively hoping they will stop the coldblooded Russian army with songs and love.

Rezo, keeping watch by the cross street, sees special army soldiers in black uniforms jump out from the tanks and close off the street. Then they stand with their backs toward the meeting.

In a second they all turn around and start to squeeze the crowd into tight circle. There is no way for anyone to get out and leave. Rezo sees that none of the protestors has yet realized the intensity of the situation.

The area is blocked by the Russian army, who hold black rubber *dubinka* (clubs) in their hands. The Russians' faces and eyes are cold and hard as icebergs.

The crowd gets confused. People scream. Some shout for family members and friends.

Rezo, Zaira, and Levan are near the open door of the movie theater. Suddenly, screams are louder. Someone opens all the front doors and lets the crowd into the building. The rushing crowd pushes Rezo, Zaira, and Levan inside ahead of it. There is little lighting, almost not enough to see the many scared boys and young and older people. Everyone huddles together, listening to the violence and screams outside. No one knows what will happen next.

Hours before, when I walked home in the late afternoon, danger was hiding treacherously in the corners of sunny streets, to painfully wake us up to the horrible reality that would permanently stay in our memories, our souls, our mentality as Georgians, and even inside of some people's bodies. The horror would define the future direction of our country on its brink of freedom. Like a brightly colored photograph marched over by an advancing army and left in tatters, memories of this day would carry spots of blood and salty tears, and never would be erased.

Who could have imagined what cruel moves the Russian government had planned?

Inside the theater, time passes until no one knows whether it is very late or early the next day. Finally, someone lets the people know they can all go out and go home. Everyone leaves the building.

Outside it is dark, a nightmare. My dad, Rezo, sees panic, fear, and bloody people running. A few people carry something heavy as they try to escape. Rezo realizes it is a wounded man.

Fear reigns in the whole area.

"Let's go, let's go!" Rezo hurries Zaira and Levan along back streets among other running people.

✿

I go to bed at midnight, thinking that for sure evil is not going to sleep this night.

Around four o'clock in the morning, Dad, Mom, and Levan arrive home. Shaken, they assure each other and Grandma and me that they are alive and whole.

Minutes later, the TV news announces the deaths of many innocent people. Across Georgia there is shock! My whole family feels lucky that each of us survived, but also feels guilt, because others were not the lucky ones last night.

Then the news announces an even bigger tragedy: The Russian army released poisoned gas into the crowd. Of the people poisoned with the chemical gas, their health has been damaged permanently.

We suddenly fear: Maybe Dad, Mom, and Levan breathed the poison too.

Aunt Thea decides to telephone her friend, Nugzar, who is director of the movie theater where Rezo, Zaira, and Levan were pushed and seemingly survived.

"Nugzar, hello. I am glad you answer the phone. Do you know if poison gas was released in your building?"

After a short conversation, the truth is revealed. The movie theater was reserved for the army to rest there after they finished their cruel mission. Whoever went inside the movie theater building was saved from poisoning.

It was the director who ordered the doors be opened for the public once he realized his countrymen had been set up for a great horror. That night the director sacrificed his position, but he saved many people's health and lives.

⚘

In the fall of 1989, Levan flies to Canada, to study at the University of British Columbia. The eye-opening and mind-flourishing experiences are incomparable. Even for a sister at home.

The year Levan spends at the University of British Columbia is like Christmas for me. Just like writing wish lists for Santa, I share my wishes by phone with my brother.

"Levan, buy Levi Strauss jeans for me, please, please!" Nothing stylish is available in the stores of Soviet Georgia. The black market can offer us anything, but prices are hardly affordable for regular citizens.

Levi Strauss jeans are the most desirable item for every Georgian teenager. Maybe some symbol is hidden in that denim dream—freedom of thought and the freedom to desire, which we are deprived of in the existing system.

Having a brother who studies at a Canadian university has also given me popularity. Only four Georgian students were sent to American and Canadian universities, so that accomplishment is something notable.

"Her brother studies in Canada!" I hear whispers as I pass through the university square. Thankfully it does not make me lose my natural humbleness, but the fact is undeniable. And everyone is waiting to see new American Levi's on me.

"Levan, I would love to have some sweaters, skirts, and T-shirts, please!" I beg him on the phone constantly.

"Maka, dear, leave him alone!" My dad always tries to silence my dreams of colorful clothing. "He doesn't have time for shopping! He has to study!"

"Levan, please buy at least something . . . cool . . . anything!" I cannot give up dreaming and hoping that he will find time for my presents. After all my school years wearing the same brown soviet uniform, I long for changes.

Levan finishes the school year with great success. He comes back to Tbilisi in June 1990. With immeasurable joy I welcome him in the airport.

Behind me I hear my mom's fearful voice whisper to my dad, "Rezo, what has he done with his hair?" She doesn't dare to ask Levan why his black hair is a little bit longer than the neat, short cut that Georgian men always wear.

It is summer break when Levan returns home, but he wants to see his teachers so he can share his Canadian experience with them. A few days after his arrival home, he visits the university campus, eager to answer the many questions his instructors must have for him.

The greetings are not what he anticipated.

"Oh, my gosh, Levan, what have you done with your hair?"

"Wow, your hair is long!"

"Wow, are you going to attend classes with that long hair in September?!"

Spending a year in a new culture has enriched Levan's outlook and approaches. But unfortunately, all of that is bombarded by the narrow-minded views of the Georgian people whose mentality has been damaged by communism.

Levan's innovative and naïve try to look even slightly different is met with confusion and incomprehension. I begin to realize *that* is how limited communism's thinking horizon is.

I begin to realize that, even more than me, Levan is stretching his wings.

※

Since Levan has started participating in the educational exchange program, my family has started interacting with students from different countries, through affiliation with exchange program students from England, Canada, and the United States.

"Mom, Eddie will be visiting Georgia for two weeks. I lived with host families while visiting England, so now it's our turn to host one of their students," Levan announces one day in his usual way of making people shocked with not-ordinary news.

"Levan!" Mom sounds perturbed. "Where is he going to live? This place will be too small for him!"

My brother quickly finds the solution. "You and dad own the condo in the Saburtalo area of Tbilisi. The condo is currently vacant. I will move there with Eddie for two weeks so he is not alone."

The night before Eddie is scheduled to arrive, the condo is freshly scrubbed, polished, and waiting for his early morning arrival. Levan is already staying there.

We have been so busy preparing the condo for Eddie that spring cleaning is barely underway in our condo, but the Saburtalo condo is ready. We will go there tomorrow to greet Eddie and show him where he will be staying.

My parents and I turn in for the night and are sleeping calmly and peacefully. Before dawn, the doorbell rings.

Levan's buddy, Tamaz, is in charge of distributing all foreign students into their host families. "Maka, open the door! I brought Eddie!" Tamaz calls from outside the front door.

In the dark I jump from the bed, search for my clothes, and run to the door, still fixing my hair. Alarmed thoughts race in my head: *Eddie was not supposed to come here! He was supposed to go to the Saburtalo condo! The house is a mess! What are we going to do now?*

Tamaz keeps knocking and ringing the bell. I open the door.

"Maka, I have to run to distribute other students. This is Eddie. He is very tired and hungry. Make sure to feed him. He's all yours to take care of."

"Tamaz, you were supposed to drop him at the condo where Levan is staying—"

But these last words were lost in the air as he disappears without any other instruction of what to do with the guest.

All right! I'd better figure things out! I tell myself. *The journey begins!*

According to Georgian hospitality and tradition, we offer food to our guests, no matter whether it is planned or not. My mom goes straight to the kitchen and takes out the whole chicken from the refrigerator. She starts to cook while I am busy setting the table. As I was taught by my grandma, I set plates and silverware for all of us, to give a more sophisticated look to the dining table.

Then I invite Eddie, "Eddie, please come to the table." It is not time for my shyness. My knowing of the English language from school, university, and my friend's charitable tutoring all come in handy for me.

It is seven in the morning, but our guest has traveled for many hours and seems very hungry. My mom brings a platter with crispy fried chicken and sets it in the middle of the table.

"Please, help yourself." Modestly I offer him the food.

"Are you going to eat?" I hear impatience in Eddie's question.

"No, we are not hungry." I reply.

My parents smile intuitively. They have no idea what we are speaking about, since the English language is a definite stranger to them.

As though relieved that the whole chicken is only for him, with a quick move Eddie relocates the bird in front of him, and, leaving us in astonishment, eats all of it.

He is eating all the chicken?! We could use a whole chicken to feed the family—four to five members of it. We could cook a whole meal: chicken in walnut sauce! Oh, no! My thoughts are confused into something unusual. At this moment, I know there will be more cultural differences to come with this student exchange program.

After we have fed Eddie, I telephone my brother. "Levan, wake up! Eddie is here. You need to pick him up and take him to settle in the condo."

"What? How come Eddie is there? Who brought him there? He was supposed to be here." Levan is confused and still half asleep.

A few hours later, Levan comes to pick up Eddie and asks me a favor. "Maka, can you please spend time with Eddie for the next two weeks instead of me? I am very busy at work. You and he will be going with group of Georgian and English students and professors to see the sights of Georgia."

Levan works and has a pretty tight schedule. "Really? Of course!" I exclaim. My curious nature senses something exciting and interesting could be awaiting me ahead.

I immediately start to imagine how I will explain to Eddie about my country's history and cultural details. I know it will be fun exploring the city with a foreigner, and, most importantly, I know that I will expand my horizon of outlook. I agree to be a tour guide, with great pleasure.

The next morning at nine o'clock, Eddie and I are ready to join the rest of the group, five students from England and five

Georgians who are Levan's friends. I know them all. We go to explore the city.

The first place the bus takes all of us is Old Tbilisi. This is the part with the most kept style and historical details. The visiting professor who is leading the group of students says, "Oh, what a unique view! I see so many churches here! So which religion are you Georgians practicing?"

Marina, one of the guide girls, answers, "Georgia is one of the oldest orthodox Christian countries, started in 337 A.D., and historically this faith has very important meaning for us. Strong belief in Christianity saved Georgia from constant wars from neighboring Muslim countries. Sultans of those countries were determined to conquer and rule in our land. And achieving that goal would be quickly possible by changing the religion among the Georgian people. That would lead to changing our traditions and language.

"Many Georgian kings and queens were tortured for that purpose and chose to die for Christianity and for their country," Marina adds. "Their willful and heroic example grew patriotism among ordinary people of Georgia. That's why you see so many churches around."

"How old is the oldest church in Georgia?" Curiosity shows itself in Helena, a lean, blonde English girl.

Tamaz replies, "Some of the early surviving churches belong to the fifth century, but we were tolerant with other religions too. Along with Christian churches, you see synagogues and Muslim mosques as well. Now these historical valuables are part of each Georgians' life.

"They are also favorite getaways for all of us," he explains. "Friends and families go visiting various monasteries and churches. Afterward we have picnics, bonfires, singing, playing on guitars, and poems read under the moonlight."

Philip seems to imagine it. "This sounds so romantic!"

Eddie's interest is awaking too. "How old is Tbilisi?"

Now it is my turn to explain. "Tbilisi, the capital of Georgia, is more than 1500 years in age. There is a legend about Tbilisi and how it was founded in the fifth century." Each Georgian child knows this legend, and we are proud to tell our guests about it. "In the fifth century, the king of Georgia, Vakhtang Gorgasali, went hunting with his men and other royals in the forest. The falcon caught a pheasant, but suddenly both the falcon and the pheasant disappeared. The king and his company went searching for the birds and found them floating in natural hot sulfur springs. The king was impressed with the discovery of this natural resource. Soon, with his order, the city was built around this area and named after the springs. *Tbili* means *warm* in Georgian."

After exploring Old Tbilisi, we drive on picturesque Rustaveli Avenue, the main prospect of the city.

"Whose statue is that?" Michael asks. The statue is of a standing man with a pointy hat.

Kathie answers, "This is Shota Rustaveli, the twelfth century writer whose epic poem *The Knight in the Panther's Skin* has withstood the test of time as a classic. Shota Rustaveli's poem is known with the same popularity in Georgia as Shakespeare's *Romeo and Juliet* is in England. The poem has been highly praised by literary critics for its language and dramatic effect. It consists of over 1600 quatrains," she adds, to many impressed expressions. "It contains much romance and highlights the strong values of love, bravery, devotion, and friendship. The creativity and romantic character of the Georgian people are expressed in this poem as well in countless poems and novels."

We talk about the amazing Caucasus mountains, the polyphonic sounds of folk songs—which distinguish them from other sounds and make them musically unique—and Georgian dances that are a proof of strong, warrior-like characteristics of Georgian men and gentle, feminine qualities of Georgian women. In those dances one can see the history of the country and the heroism, bravery, and patriotism of its people.

Most of all, our English visitors and we Georgians talk together about the most exceptional gift Georgians have to offer—our hospitality.

At the dinner table, talk continues about the uniqueness of our country. The topic turns to the ancient art of wine making. Professor Tamara shares her knowledge on the subject with the whole group.

"Wine making began in Georgia seven thousand years ago. As historians and archeologists are proving, grape seeds were found in Caucasian tombs, along with wine implements such as wine vessels. Nowhere else has been found the evidence of a wine-making culture as old as the one in Georgia. Even the word *wine* itself has been traced to the Georgian word *gvino*."

For me, the two weeks I serve as tour guide of my country are unforgettable, and I have many new experiences. More and more I feel the joy of stretching my wings.

Chapter Four
After Collapse of the Soviet Union

In June 1991, Levan graduates from TSU.

The very next morning, he is assigned to work in the Ministry of Foreign Affairs of Georgia, with the recommendations of his university professors. His language skills are incomparable.

He finds the work interesting and intense, since many changes are happening.

The Soviet Union is struggling. In August 1991, radical political forces attempt a coup in Moscow to overthrow President Mikhail Gorbachev. Although they are defeated, it still leaves a political crisis. In December 1991, the Soviet Union collapses after a seventy-year rule, and with it the Cold War ends.

The wind of changes has already started blowing over Europe and the United States, restructuring everything. The changes have been especially outstanding for people from the fifteen countries that had been under the Soviet Union.

Not surprisingly, the communists' downfall tenses the situation in the newly independent republics. Soon this causes more crises.

Throughout this intense situation, Levan interacts with and interprets for diplomatic figures during negotiations. He interprets for Georgian President Shevardnadze and all political figures visiting our country. The most important political visitor he interprets for is James Baker, the United States Secretary of State.

One morning Levan wakes up early and starts to get ready. "I am leaving," he calls on his way out the door. "A limo is picking me up."

My mom and I run to the bedroom window that overlooks the street, curious and anxious to see what is going on. And there it is! A black stretch limousine is waiting for Levan. Each morning since then, the limo has driven up and waits for Levan in front of our condo entrance.

The first day the limo arrives for Levan, it takes all day for the excitement to calm down. As soon as it does, Levan comes home with amazing news.

We all sit at the dinner table. Mom brings our favorite dish, chicken in walnut sauce. Corn flour mamaliga—Georgian corn bread—steams nearby, warm from out of the oven, and delicious Sulguni cheese melts inside the hot poultry.

Levan calmly slides his fork under a slice of the mamaliga, takes a piece, and then says, "Mom, Dad, I'm the interpreter for the opening ceremony of the American Embassy in Georgia. The ceremony will be at the Metechi Palace Hotel."

Mom, Dad, and I stare at each other in wonder.

Then Levan turns toward me. "Maka, I am allowed to bring one guest. Would you like to, please, escort me there?"

I find my voice. "Wait a minute," I say with a huge grin. "Is that question even necessary? Of course, of course!" Under the table, my feet dance with happiness.

"After the ceremony," Levan tells me, "there will be a reception on the hotel's top floor, overlooking all of Tbilisi. And you will see so many significant people!"

"Oh, okay, I'll have to find a dress for that day." In my mind I am already getting ready for the event.

A few days later, a shiny white stretch limousine arrives down in front of our condominium for Levan and me. From their windows, the whole neighborhood is watching the excitement.

I wear a long gray skirt, which I bought when I went into East Germany on a tour, and a white blouse. My soul flies from inner happiness.

"Maka, are you ready?" Levan asks. "We need to leave." He opens the front door.

I kiss my mom who herself is all in smiles from happiness.

☙

The Metechi Palace Hotel—the first modern hotel, built within the last few years—has wide windows and contemporary architecture that single it out from the rest of the buildings in the city. It is prestigious, modern, exciting, and new! Something *new*!

A glass elevator—*glass!*—is taking people to the top floor. I enter the elevator with a bright smile on my face.

Among others there, I meet Mr. Gela Charkviani, a Georgian diplomat and the number-one English language specialist in Georgia.

"So who are you?" he asks me.

"My name is Maka. I am escorting the interpreter. He is my brother." I feel proud to be among such well-educated and well-known people.

"It is nice to meet you, Maka. I am honored to say that your brother Levan is the second-best interpreter in Georgia after me!"

I smile at his compliment of Levan and his humor. I am certain I'll never forget these words of Gela Charkviani.

During the ceremony, the ambassador talks while Levan interprets. Then others give speeches. All of that is followed by drinks and appetizers. With a glass of champagne in my hand, I greet, meet, talk, and share my thoughts with others.

I know this celebration of the American Embassy will be one of the most elevated moments in my life.

※

Freedom arises with the collapse of the USSR, but sadly it also sends people into misperception. Georgian leaders try to figure out which way to take our newly independent country. Political confusion and tense relationships between Georgian opposition parties lead to civil war.

Shootings start on December 22, 1991, right in downtown Tbilisi. Georgians fighting against Georgians.

The day begins regularly, though.

Around noon I go to the dentist's office to pull out my troubled tooth. I enter the clinic very scared, since I have heard many cruel stories about the dentists who relentlessly remove teeth from people. The nurse leads me to a room with greenish paint on the walls. The plastic dentist chair is as cold as the nurse's face.

With an emotionless expression, the nurse injects a needle into my gum to make it numbed, but it feels like someone is driving a nail into my jawbone. It is a torture, but sadly it is only one existing norm.

My tooth begins to buzz. The nurse, still not showing any emotion, prepares tools. Then the doctor starts his job.

Suddenly we hear voices shouting. Outside is an armed group of young men.

"They are coming! They are coming!" someone in the clinic shouts. "They are starting the fight!"

Everyone in the office becomes panicked. "Hurry up!" the doctor orders the nurse. His face is scared. "We need to extract her tooth!"

"Open your mouth!" the nurse yells at me. "We don't have much time! They are coming!"

Each of us is in complete shock, none of us acting consciously, but rather by instinct.

I open my mouth, the doctor and nurse start pulling at my tooth. It isn't fully anesthetized yet. I feel the twisting, cracking, and pain. Then finally, the cruelty is over.

I jump from the chair and run outside with everyone else. Terrified and in horrible pain, I run toward home.

Streets are blocked by many military vehicles and barriers. No transportation is available.

I run through people's yards like others are doing, anything to escape from the new war zone. Thankfully, my house is just fifteen minutes away. I arrive home, in pain from the injection and pulled tooth, but safe.

Safe.

☙

During the next ten days, the city appears to be empty of life. No one dares to go out. Only the chatter of bullets fired between Georgians downtown disturbs the dead quiet.

The combatants wield their guns mercilessly, destroying architecturally valuable buildings. In the end of this madness, Tbilisi's famous historical art gallery is burnt to ashes.

School #1, which over the decades has counted many famous people among its students, is riddled with bullets. Old Hotel

Tbilisi, beautiful for its European architectural style, is destroyed so badly that it will face demolition.

Our briefly promising future is snuffed out by the dramatic events, which will certainly leave a path of destruction behind for years.

☙

New Year's night of 1992 goes by unremarkably, as does Christmas. With our Orthodox Christian calendar, it is on January 7.

TV channels stopped working during the past ten days of the civil war. Only news on the radio is available. Scared people wait for more disaster.

My brother has had to work, no matter the conditions, and my parents have been terrified since Levan has to drive toward the hotbed of violence.

Suddenly, on January 8, TV broadcasting resumes. That same evening, the telephone rings.

"Rezo, is that your son, Levan, on TV?" an excited voice asks.

Dad is amazed. "Levan is on TV?!"

He hangs up the phone. Then all three of us, my parents and I, rush to turn on the TV. On the screen we see Levan in a green pullover sweater, sitting among political figures. The distinctive and memorable color of his sweater is like a symbol of hope after many dark days full of fear.

Next to Levan is sitting the newly nominated prime minister of Georgia. We see other important political figures and international journalists, who are holding microphones and cameras, impatiently waiting for an explanation of current events.

Mom, Dad, and I are trying to hold in our excitement, happiness, pride, and hope for improvements and a peaceful future, along with our confusion.

"What? What is going on?"

"Oh, my goodness?! Levan is sitting next to the new-elected vice president?"

"What is he doing there? What is going on? Is the war over?"

Yes! We learn that the war is over!

Levan has been called to interpret at a press conference on live TV for the vice president and reporters from other countries. The whole of Georgia is watching TV at this moment.

Hours later evening comes, and our phone hasn't stopped ringing since the televised press conference. For those who know Levan, the phone calls are a double joy—the war is over, and many people see Levan as a hope for the future of Georgia.

Eventually my brother's talent gets noticed by an American physicist and philanthropist while she visits Georgia on a political tour, which Levan interprets.

She and her husband offer to pay for Levan's continuing education at the University of British Columbia, since Levan was already accepted there but hasn't had enough money to cover the remaining years of travel, educational, and living costs.

Accepting their philanthropic gift, Levan returns to Canada.

※

After seventy years of being ruled, the abruptly regained independence causes the Georgian people and other former soviet nations to experience confusion, disappointment, fear, and even other civil wars.

The old ways of living have been wiped out. People now need to familiarize themselves with capitalistic ways, which are foreign to them.

The doors of new opportunities have opened up. Each of our fifteen small nations have gained independence and treasured freedom so that we might flourish in the free world, but at a high cost. People are unprepared for such a transformation. Today's generations have never experienced capitalism or free thinking.

In a communistic system, jobs are given to people, salaries are set on a monthly basis, and no one has to show their best potential. But now Georgian people face a new reality. They have to think about making a living for their own families.

But the civil war and outside political condition has taken a toll on Georgia's economy. Ruined downtown is frightening. Jobs in cities across the country are vanishing, and villages are losing signs of life entirely. Young people come to Tbilisi in search of work, but Tbilisi is incapable of satisfying even its residents.

Yet, it is vital to have some income to survive. People must think of creating their own businesses.

The first signs of new business ideas start to appear. The most visible are small metal booths, which hardly fit one person inside. These soon multiply and cover the whole city. These booths are meager hope in a dark new reality.

Tbilisi becomes "the city of booths." They are everywhere, no pattern, no style. They are unpainted, soon to be covered with rust, since no one can afford to buy paint.

And what are these booths for? They are mini stores that resell from one place to another the simplest items of daily use, such as cigarettes, soap, matches, lighters, salt, a few loaves of bread a day, sunflower seeds, chewing gum. As miserable as it sounds, these are the most demanded items among the customers.

My dad continues to work at the Writers' Union. He isn't getting paid, since most organizations, just like the Writers' Union, had been government funded. And the government is dead.

But he still continues to work hard on his future books, hoping that someday better times will come and his dedication will be appreciated.

My mom decides to contribute some income. "Rezo, I will work in a booth and make some money. Working hours are pretty long, from eight in the morning until eight at night, and the salary is very insignificant and miserable."

Compared with American value, she will earn about $2 for twelve hours of work.

"Zaira, are you sure you want to do that?" Dad is uneasy about these working terms for his wife.

But Mom insists. "It is not much money, and we really can't buy much with it, maybe just bread for a day. But there is not much to choose from either." Mom's voice is firm.

∅

Across Georgia, this becomes a lonely and gloomy time. Young people, full of talent and energy, struggle the most. The future is dark. Nothing interesting, nothing soul- and mind-enriching, is out there. No events, no opportunities, no jobs.

Nothing. Nothing is there.

The only change in this dormant life is marriage. Not just dating or a boyfriend-girlfriend period, but the marriage itself.

According to Georgian cultural traditions, young people's relationships must remain limited prior to marriage. This is made worse during communism, when true feelings are not appreciated.

Even more so, they are lost. Everything is based on lies, but the most horrible is lying to self.

If a young couple wants to take their relationship to the next step, there is only one solution—marriage. But many times they are not even sure how they feel about each other.

In my family we already had an example of society's judgements. My aunt, a beautiful, highly educated, talented woman, had a label: unmarried. Unfortunately, she passed away young, but the pain of the judgement she lived with pressured me growing up that I should get married as soon as I turned eighteen.

I am now twenty-two. And everything around me is collapsing: the country's miserable conditions, my parents working all day, my brother away in Canada, all my best friends married, and canceled classes. I am unable to change my unbearable reality. And this feeling is making me depressed.

Definitely my mom worries about me.

It's a cold October day. I stand wrapped in my coat, waiting to catch the bus.

"Hello," a man's voice says.

I turn and see the familiar face of David, my best friend's cousin. "Hi."

"How are you Maka? Where are you going?"

"Actually I am going to your sister's neighborhood, to see a tailor. She is sewing a new coat for me."

"May I accompany you?"

I know he has had affection for me, but I do not think of him in the same way. We have very different personalities. However, life is so empty and boring that company sounds exciting. "Okay."

We spend the day together. In the following week, we start talking on the phone to each other. Soon he asks me for a date.

Let it be! There is nothing better going on in this dark and miserable life!

We start to date.

I have known David for almost two years. We went on a trip to Sankt Petersburg, Russia, the year before, with a group of students from the university. After that trip we knew we weren't a match.

But now, after a very short dating time, David asks me to be his wife. He offers to elope.

I agree.

One Saturday evening for a date, we just go to his place. According to Georgian mentality, the next morning I am claimed as a married woman.

The same traditions rule me to live in his house, where his mother and father have lived for the last thirty years. So on a seventh floor, in a two-bedroom apartment, my next chapter as a married woman starts.

Married life feels like a roller coaster, right from the first day.

Georgian mothers' emotional attachments to their growing sons often become challenging after sons get married. Jealousy, controlling position, and being in charge at the house causes problems with daughters-in-law. Sons end up in the middle of the battles, not knowing how to love and respect mothers and wives at the same time, as well not allowing them to take advantage of each other.

Our rushed decision to get married is further tested by economic and political situations, unemployment, inability to take care of the family, lack of love, and lack of common values. These reasons all play a big role in dissolving many marriages of my generation.

Even with those challenges, I finish work on my master's degree in linguistics, or as we refer to it, philology. In the summer of 1993, I pass the last exam and complete my education.

"I have the diploma! I am free! I can work now!"

※

The next morning my dad's writer friend, whom I have known for most of my childhood, calls my dad. "Rezo, can Maka work for my literary newspaper *The Word*?"

Of course! Why would I not? That is my field of interest!

But there is one problem. I am a married woman, and my mother-in-law is not very happy with the idea that I would be working.

"You are a married woman now!" she announces to me. "You can't spend so much time outside of this family, or visiting your family and friends!"

That came as thunder to my head! "What?! Because I am married, I can't see my parents, friends, or go to work?"

I have a character trait—the more someone tries to forbid me freedom, the more I am going to strive to my purpose or goal.

So I know I will work for sure!

And the next morning, all excited for the new job, I leave home. A fifteen-minute bus ride, and I am here!

The Communist, the publishing house located in downtown Tbilisi, is the biggest publisher in Georgia. The idea of having a job in the middle of life flow makes my heart beat with excitement. The publishing house is a four-floor building with glass windows. I stand in front of it and stare.

Finally, I push the huge, heavy glass door and enter the building . . . and with it a promising, bright future, an interesting and fascinating life!

This place is full of everything. A variety of newspapers. Book and magazine stands. People exchanging information. The smell of printing ink. Smoke from cigarettes. Dust from the streets. The noise of transportation. A florist sitting in the corner selling wildflowers and calling people to buy them, "Flowers for your loved ones! Flowers for your loved ones!" Mothers holding their children by the hand and racing somewhere in the early morning. Young couples in love standing and staring at each other. People greeting, meeting, and talking.

Everything that would make me happy is here: people, noise, motion, and life excitement. And me!

Interacting with famous writers and creative people feels somewhat natural. I am about to find myself surrounded with books again, like my summers with my family at Kvishkheti.

Wow. I'm working here! I'll come here every morning to read poems, stories, articles to edit, and so much more."

The noise of the printing machines sounds like an airplane engine. Newspapers in Georgia are still printed in mechanical style. Enormous machines cast words and sentences from lead and print them onto paper.

For few weeks, going to work is so joyous. But, sadly, literary publications cannot survive long in a country in economic freefall. *The Word* does not survive either.

Instead, it is time for politics. Soon I get a new offer, to edit content for a newspaper called *The Chronicles*. It is owned by an opposition political party—a newborn kid of liberated society.

My job is less exiting, since I have to read and edit political and informational articles. But my explorer spirit still adds some excitement to it: I start translating small articles from English into Georgian.

Soon motherhood stops my career. Temporarily, I think at first. But as political, economic, and social conditions continue going down the hill toward the eventual, inevitable collision, I realize there is no way back to a normal, flourishing life anymore. In this time of hardship, I become a mother to a son. We name him Levan, after my brother, who still lives in Canada.

It is May 1994. I am twenty-four. The Soviet Union has been dissolved for two and a half years. Living conditions are challenging but still surmountable. But truly hard times are about to come.

✿

In the fall of 1994, when Levan is almost six months old, complete decline begins. From this time on, "the normal life" becomes a fairy tale. Chaos engulfs the country.

Today starts as a regular November day. My mom wakes up as usual, around seven in the morning. Little Levan and I are living for this time with my parents. According again to Georgian traditions, when the first baby is born, the mom and newborn move to the mom's parents' house so her mother can help to raise her child in the beginning months. After several months, they move back to the husband's house, where they all live together with the in-laws. So for now I am at my parents' house with my little son. Levan and I are still asleep.

Mom goes to kitchen to make breakfast. She fills the kettle with water and puts it on the old gas stove. From a small box hanging on the wall she withdraws a match.

Everything is so natural to her. She had done this many times in her life, the same exact routine. Soon water will be boiling, and she will be setting the tea for my dad, herself, and me.

She lights a match with her right hand. With her left she turns the handle of the stove. She brings the flame closer to the round metal burner, where the cooking gas usually comes out.

"Hmm, what's going on?" she mumbles with confusion.

"Hmm, what's going on?" This same sentence probably echoes this morning in every kitchen in the city.

Mom tries again. And again. And again. Nothing!

This is so confusing that she cannot even figure out what is happening.

"Where is the gas? What is going on?"

The phone calls start, to each other, to the Gas Department. Nothing! Only confusion.

Soon the rough reality becomes clearer—Russia, big provider of natural gas for Georgia and other former soviet republics, is trying to teach us a lesson for being naughty and recalcitrant. They have shut off the gas supply to Georgia.

"This is Russia's payback for losing Georgia and other republics. They'll do anything to harm us!" This is the conclusion made by thousands.

Little do we know that this is just the beginning of the misery that Russia has planned for us.

"Oh, let's wait a little! They will open the pipes, and we'll be able to cook!" My mom tries to close eyes to our unpleasant reality. "Until then, we can eat leftovers."

Luckily, I still breastfeed Levan. But what about us? Hours pass by, and there is no sign of comfort cooking.

"Maka, let's go into the basement," Mom finally says. "We have canned food that I made for winter." She realizes we have to start using reserved supplies.

Since my parents live on a first floor, wooden stairs go down into a cold room located right underneath the kitchen. I open the cover and go down. Every family in Georgia keeps homemade canned vegetables for winter.

The shelves are filled with jars of canned eggplants, pickles, pickled tomatoes, tomato paste, and the Georgian signature plum sauce *Tkemali*, which deliciously goes with any type of meat, fried potato, or just by itself. Also there are plenty of fruit jams and fruit preserves.

I choose a few jars and hand them to Mom.

"This should be enough!" Mom says confidently.

We eat, and for some time everything is good, although Mom lights matches every few hours to see if the gas is working.

No sign.

Eventually hours turn into days. Russia does not change his brutal decision.

I have grown worried watching the food inside the refrigerator become less and less. Then one day I have to say the words, "We have no food left in the refrigerator."

Soon the pantry runs out of supplies. Our only remaining hope is the basement.

"Zaira, do you have some bread?" Our next-door neighbor, Aunt Ira, calls us from the balcony.

Neighborhood is very special for us. We help each other, visit often, and give encouragement when needed. Now, in this hard time especially, we need support from one another.

Four days pass slowly and dreadfully, as no one wants to accept the fact that we have no way to cook. Finally, we realize we have to figure out other ways to feed ourselves.

On the fourth day, when most of the supplies are gone, Nodar, our fourth-floor neighbor, has an idea. He says, "We need to make a bonfire in the yard." Nodar seems very confident in his idea.

"How are we going to make a fire?" Aunt Ira's husband, Irakli, a fifty-year-old man, is concerned. "We have no wood."

"We will use tires," Nodar explains.

"Tires?"

"Yes, car tires, rubber tires. They burn well. Obviously, we need to eat."

Aunt Ira reaches out to my mom from the balcony that connects us. "Hey, Zaira, bring whatever you can cook, and an old pot that you would not care if it is ruined, and let's cook on a fire."

Others call out to more neighbors, and soon the yard is inspired with new life. Everyone carries their share of pots and food. Some gather any wood they can find. Since Tbilisi residents live mostly in condominiums, it is impossible to find firewood, so people start bringing old furniture, broken boards, anything that will burn. Within hours, the city's yards are lit with fires to cook food and feed the children.

From this day on, the capital city looks like a big chimney, as smoke is everywhere, much of it black from the burning tires. But from those smoky times there is still a good outcome. People are closer, more helpful, and more caring of each other. And sometimes our evenings end up with songs together around bonfires.

The winter will only get tougher. We have to survive some way. The natural gas is not coming back.

People start to dig out long-forgotten heating supplies from their basements. We make use of old kerosene stoves, kerosene lamps, kerosene heaters, and kerosene oil. Months later, cooking with gas is a long-lost dream.

Then one day we find ourselves in a bigger shock: The electricity is shut off.

☙

"We need candles. Do we have any candles?" Mom runs to a small store right at the corner of our street and buys candles, matches, and canned food, just in case. She doesn't buy much, though. "Tomorrow everything will be back to normal!"

People try to keep hope with saying such things, although something inside many of us is already giving dreadful signs of more problems to come.

Difficulties grow with a chain reaction. The absence of gas and electricity cause the loss of hot water and heat.

The abnormal has become the new normal. Many trees are cut down in villages and even around the cities. Clearly, it is impossible to think about ecology when people have physical existence to worry about. But soon the tragic outcome becomes clear, especially in the countryside. With no windbreaker around the fields, heavy winds damage the crops.

The miseries do not stop. More come that we did not imagine or dream of.

The hardest to deal with is the shortage of bread—an important source of survival. Since electricity is cut off, and the import and export of goods are affected by unsettled, disordered economic times, bakeries are able to bake only limited amount, or nothing at all.

Everyone needs bread—at least for children, for older people—at least the bread! Outside the stores, devastated people form lines to buy bread starting at midnight, even though stores do not open until eight o'clock in the morning. On cold winter nights, for countless hours, Mom and others stand freezing in the darkness. We all take turns, but Mom freezes the most, since mostly I stay with my son, while Dad's health cannot take the freezing cold.

Health definitely is something we have to worry about. Our inability to call for a doctor or buy medicine would demolish our already unbearable lives even more.

※

Disasters do not stop coming. Who would imagine that all the bank savings and retirement pensions would disappear, leaving the country's economy disabled? My parents, like everyone else, lose the family accounts they had in the bank.

When my brother and I were children, Mom often said, "When Rezo and I stop working, I want to have a happy, stress-free retirement." And she put away savings from the monthly salary. Now their dreams and hopes are greatly dashed.

Next, the currency is devalued. Then, due to fraudsters, banks are soon left without money entirely.

It is in this hardship that we reach spring.

The chain reaction of bad events keeps rolling and rolling.

The next cataclysm? Disappearance of jobs. From a traditional perspective, the burden of responsibility lies heavily on men. This has a huge emotional impact, since Georgian pride instructs them to make a living and take care of their families. But finding a job in most cases is unsuccessful, since almost no jobs exist.

The stress from these unfortunate attempts to find work affect relationships, leading to many divorces.

Women, on the other hand, start taking greater responsibility as mothering instincts awake in them. Everyone's effort is needed, regardless of gender, status, or age.

Destruction has touched every part of life. The quality of education in schools and universities has plummeted, since frozen classrooms and lack of books are not good supporters for youth.

Children now worry about things they should not worry in a functioning society.

⌀

After many months, periodic electricity returns, and with it hot water! Joyful shouts are heard everywhere. People quickly jump into showers, all excited: "Hot water's coming! We can take a shower in a civilized way again!"

But the electricity is not sufficient to heat water for so many apartments. When everyone rushes to wash at once, the electricity soon goes out of order, or overuse causes water heaters to burn.

Often when we are lucky enough to be under a steaming shower, unexpectedly the hot water shuts off. People covered with shampoo and soap continue to rinse with shockingly cold water. We hear screams of distress, words of anger, calls for help . . . and then mothers, wives, brothers, husbands, anyone will carry in buckets of spare hot water, and the person in shower uses small cupfuls to rinse the best they can.

To make matters worse, right in the middle of taking a shower, when the electricity goes, as it often does, then there are cries for candles as well as warm rinsing water. The way condominiums are designed, bathrooms are in the middle of the condominium, so they don't have windows.

Sometime later, the cold water disappears too.

※

After few months of hell with no water, whoever is in charge gives us a rough schedule. Water might come for two to four hours per day.

Then there are calls between families. "Water has come, collect water. Hurry up!"

No light. No heat. No hot water. No cold water. Just darkness.

In this misery, I become pregnant again.

At this time David, sixteen-month-old Levan, and I live in my parents' vacant condo, in the Saburtalo area. David works twelve-hour shifts at the gas station, and I am mostly alone with my son.

The pregnancy is proceeding well, so I don't go for an ultrasound until the end of the second trimester. Finally, we decide to find out the gender of our second child. I make an appointment with a doctor who has an impeccable reputation. Confident of his professionalism, Mom and I go to his office. David, as usual, has to work.

After a short wait in hallway, I am called in.

"Hello." Dr. Svanidze smiles at me and points to the bed. There are four students in the room, discussing some case together. In a few minutes, my round belly is ready for my procedure.

Oh, my goodness! Soon I will know if I will have a boy or a girl! The exciting thought runs around in my mind. I am nervous at the same time. I lie still as Dr. Svanidze performs the ultrasound and talks with the students. The students frequently reply to him. Clearly they are still discussing a case.

I hear the words "twins," "two heads," "two hearts," "four small hands," and "four feet."

Well, I think, *the students are certainly getting trained.*

Finally, with a smile on his face, the doctor looks at me and says, "Great! You are free to go. Good luck!"

The smile on my face freezes. I am confused. With a murmur I dare to ask, "But, Doctor, . . . what about me? Are you going to tell me about my baby?"

Dr. Svanidze looks at me with astonishment. "Your baby?! Who do you think I've been talking about all this time?"

"To whom? To me? But you were talking about twins and two babies."

"And those are your babies. They're boys."

"My babies?!" For the second time, I freeze. With huge fear in my eyes, I look toward my mother. I see shock in her eyes too.

Visions of my life's upcoming reality crash into my mind like lightning bolts: the realization that in about three months I will have three little boys, that David is never home, that we have a troubled marriage, chaotic and unacceptable living conditions. . . .

The interns try to comfort us, telling us that everything will be great, but I am so terrified that it takes me quite some time until I can even move.

Dr. Svanidze takes control over the situation. He makes jokes and encourages us. The students are so caring and understanding too. The kind nurses finally help Mom and me to overcome the news. Soon after, we leave the office with relief and hope.

Chapter Five
Greater Challenges

Spring of 1996 goes by quietly. David's job at the gas station is quite worrisome, though. Hectic life conditions have affected people's attitudes. Men, especially, are very tense, on the edge. One wrong word and a fight can start.

Gas stations are dangerous places to work. One man who was rushing his sick wife to the hospital did not even have money to purchase gas. Devastated from the inability, he poured gasoline on himself right in front of people and burned himself to death.

There are also many threats and cases of robberies. Cigarettes have become dangerous as well.

Smoking is now a big problem in Georgia. People try to let their sorrow go with smoking, so having cigarettes is crucial. But smokers cannot afford to buy the tobacco diversions. By nature, Georgians have been very generous—it was almost a tradition to ask a stranger in the street for a cigarette, and everyone used to be gracious and share—but when money became unavailable, cigarettes "turned into gold." They are now the cause for many fights and even deadly encounters.

David works in this stressful environment for twelve-hour days, for insufficient salary. This has led him to drinking and depression, which affects our already cracked relationship. At the same time, our personalities and characters still do not match.

I continue to manage the family and my pregnancy anyway. This last month has been going well. Everyone accepts the fact that soon I will be the mother of three.

One night, two weeks before I am due, I wake up at night for the bathroom. I return to bed, sit on the edge of the mattress, and find myself unable to lift up my legs to lie down.

In fact, I suddenly can no longer feel my legs at all.

"David, wake up! I can't move my legs! I can't even feel them!"

The fear is absolutely dreadful. I feel like the sky is falling on me. Then life episodes start fast-forwarding in front of my eyes. I see the worst possibilities. Petrifying images smother me. "David, I can't move my legs!"

Alarmed, David dials my gynecologist, Dr. Sinauridze.

"I will meet you in the hospital at nine in the morning" is the short but firm answer from the other end of the phone.

When morning comes, I am able to get up and walk very slowly. Going down the stairs is not easy, but finally I reach David's old car and we drive to hospital.

Dr. Sinauridze is already waiting for us. He is worried about the situation.

We watch the doctor, breathless from dread while he checks me.

Then he lets out a sigh of relief, and we see some hope in his eyes. "You need to stay in the hospital, let us take care of you and the babies. Medicines and IV will help the problem you have."

The condition could have been really serious, the doctor explains. The heavy weight of pregnancy is unequal for my light weight of body. That can cause opening of the pelvic bone, which can lead women to disability.

I pray and praise God, for that is not my case.

The improvement is noticeable from the second day. I slowly start to lift my legs again.

My due date of May 22 is coming soon, but the twins might also arrive early. Dr. Sinauridze is scheduled to be on call on May 22, and something inside of me tells me that I will deliver on that exact day.

It is the morning of May 22. The nurse checks my condition and sends me to the labor department. Soon pain starts and increases gradually. I am supposed to be in this room until the actual birth process starts.

Suddenly I hear a big noise, as if someone is trying to break the front door in.

"Where is the doctor? We need the doctor! A woman is dying!" A man's demanding voice is giving the orders.

"I am the doctor," I hear, "but I can't leave the facility. I am on call."

"We don't care! You have to come with us!"

I hear the fearful murmurs of the nurses. I look through my partly open door and see two men pointing automatic guns at the doctor.

Nothing and no one moves, only the two gunmen. They force the doctor to go, leaving everyone in complete shock.

In a shaky voice, a nurse says he is being taken to a village two hours' drive from Tbilisi. No one knows when he might be back.

A few hours go by. My pain becomes more frequent.

"I think labor has started!" I call out, terrified.

The nurses are still so unsteady from the events that no one comprehends my words. "It's okay. It's not time yet. You are okay." They all try to calm me down, not paying much attention to my begging for help.

But I can feel that the first baby is trying to come out.

No one seems to care.

Suddenly an unearthly scream breaks out from me.

That seems to awaken the nurses from their disconnected state, and they realize they have some duties to take care of.

One checks me. "The babies are coming!" she yells to her assistants. Then she tells me, "Hurry, get up! We need to move you to a laboring table!"

The nurses help me to get up. It seems to me that I am running with unearthly speed, but in fact I can hardly move. The nurses help me climb onto a labor table, and in the same exact second that I lie down, a little baby slides out.

Thankfully the nurses have gathered their wits. One catches the baby. A heartbeat later, Dr. Sinauridze runs to my bed and gives me encouraging advice. Everything happens within seconds.

A healthy and cute baby boy, Sandro, has been born.

Ten minutes later contractions start again. Without any problem, Nika, another cute boy, arrives in this world.

The nurses gently place these tiny bundles on my chest. I am still in shock from my shouting experience when no one seemed to care, but I have just a little power left inside of me to feel the happiness.

I am the mother of three boys!

℘

The joyful break from sadness does not last. The months of summer become the nightmare no one wants to live through. I am blessed with three small boys, but we have no income in the family, and so no money to live on. No electricity. No hot water. Cold water only by limited hours.

It is no condition for babies. And like most new parents of twins, I have no rest.

Because I need help raising three boys, my sons and I move to my parents' home. David does also. But soon his pride as a Georgian man is shaken by living with in-laws, even though living here means to stay alive. He stubbornly moves out and starts living in his own place. This makes our chore of taking care of the babies unbearably difficult.

Awful things and good things seem to alternate in coming to us, as if passing through a revolving door. Good then bad, good then bad.

But soon, something good comes to us. One of our relatives with a job in a poultry and dairy company is able to supply us with meat and milk products. Through his help, we make it day by day through this toughest time!

In September 1996, more good comes. In the newspaper an article appears that my father wrote. It is about a previously forbidden topic—the Communist Party's repressions, and Josef Stalin's persecution of millions. We feel such joy that we can now talk about such things in our homes!

As the newspaper rests on the table, the telephone rings.

My mom answers the phone. "Hello? Yes, Rezo is here. Just one moment." She passes the handset to my dad.

She and I do not pay much attention to the phone call. We are so busy with the babies.

"Yes," my dad says. "Yes. Thank you very much." He quickly finishes the conversation. Then he starts getting ready to go.

My mom looks at him curiously. "Where are you going, Rezo?"

"To the publishing house. Something about my article." Without any more words, he leaves.

Mom and I continue our constant work of caring for the boys.

In about two hours, Dad returns home. The happy smile on his face tells us something interesting is happening.

"I got paid the royalty, eighty rubles for my article! We have money, at least for some time!"

"What? They paid you the royalty?" Mom couldn't believe his words!

"Oh, my God! This is so wonderful!" I jump about from excitement.

It wasn't too much money, maybe forty American dollars. But for a long time in Georgia all salaries have been canceled, and the bank accounts wiped out. So this money is like sunshine through a cloudy sky.

We can't buy much with it, but it is a big enough amount to make us happy. Together we make plans, think of a better life, and hope for more good to come. At this moment nothing more matters.

※

The royalties Dad has earned from writing the newspaper article becomes a turning point. It is like a sign to go on. The small amount of money gives me power to think positively.

I have longed for some changes, for improvement. I have known something has to be done to break us out from the circle which promises only more misery.

One day an idea hits my mind. The condo our family owns in the Saburtalo area of Tbilisi, and where Eddie from England stayed during the two weeks of the exchange program, is vacant. With the tough times, we have needed to live together and take care of each other, so we haven't thought of it much.

"Dad, Mom, we can't continue to live in these conditions any longer. David struggles to make a living, and isn't earning a lot. I need to change something. I have an idea!"

My parents look at me with confused faces.

"Let's rent out the Saburtalo condo. I'll remodel, prepare for tenants, and I'll manage it."

My parents consider this. Then, to my surprise, they agree to the idea.

The next morning I feed the babies, kiss them and their grandparents good-bye, drop little Levan in a day care, and head straight to the condo to figure out what needs to be done before I will show it to possible tenants.

Well, the old wallpaper in the family room doesn't look good at all. And there are more details that need to be fixed. I make a short list and, with very little money in my pocket, go to the market. The market is the street where people stand in the sunshine and rain. A few sell construction materials.

I buy some supplies. The next morning Dad and I are boiling glue for the wallpaper. I climb a ladder while my dad holds it, then I glue the paper on the walls. By the end of the day we are exhausted, but the room is refashioned.

I do some painting next, and in a few days the place is remodeled. Soon after, tenants move in, and we have a small but solid income to live on!

The project has turned out successful. That gives me the hope that I can try something else.

The Vake condominium we live in is on the first floor, and we are fortunate to have a basement under it. I think, *If we hire workers and extend that space, we will have a room that I can rent out again and bring more income.*

And that is what I do.

We slowly start to get on our feet!

David always stays away from these projects. His pride does not allow him to admit that I have abilities that are helping, or join me in increasing our chances to have a better life.

The revolving door in our lives keeps turning. With bad weather comes more difficulty.

My parents and I continue to take care of three small, energetic boys, and our energy slowly drains. As the weather gets colder, the conditions become unbearable. Diapers are a luxury. I have only one big package, for an emergency or for doctors' visits, given by my friend Lika as a gift when the twins were born. On a regular basis, fabric diapers are not fun to rewash. All the laundry is a huge obstacle. We wash it with cold water and hang it outside to dry. In winter that is hard since the laundry does not dry fast.

This winter is harsh. We are exhausted, and my dad becomes terribly sick with the flu. Soon it turns into pneumonia.

It is March 1997, and we are falling apart.

The door revolves again.

Miraculously, my mom's friend, Aunt Nino, stops by to say hello. When she finds us in misery—three adults completely incapable taking care the infants—she says, "Okay, I see what's going on here. Don't worry anymore! I am here to help. I don't ask for money. You need someone to help you get through this!"

Right away Aunt Nino takes over, not even waiting until one of us says something. "I am going to cook soup for you." Soon the house smells delicious.

For many days Aunt Nino washes piles of dirty clothes in cold water, takes care of the children, cooks and feeds us, and encourages us.

That spring of 1997, Aunt Nino saves us, three adults and three babies. The boys love step-grandma, and she has become a friend to us all. Kindness in exchange for nothing. God bless her for such humanity!

The door turns. It brings great joy. And then it brings greater challenges.

Chapter Six
Braving Unfamiliar Paths

Years have gone by since the collapse of the Soviet Union, but life has not improved. Jobs are limited and conditions still are dreadful. Sadly, people have started to accept the diminished life as normal. Some fight it, but others have given up, and many are now depressed.

It is autumn 1997. The twins are eighteen months old, and Levan is exactly two years older. Our conditions are unbearable. We are all exhausted.

David is now living in his parents' apartment. He tries to run a small grocery shop business, which means buying from one major supplier and selling to small stores. Many people do this for business. In the long run, this is only moving groceries from place to place, but at least it keeps the mind occupied, and people think they are doing something productive.

Winter is approaching. David works just two weeks out of each month. The insufficient income does not feed the family. This makes David depressed. He drinks a lot and smokes cheap cigarettes.

This definitely doesn't help our marriage and relationship. We fight and argue. David finally drops his classes at the university as he thinks it is unrealistic to even try. I don't agree, but I can't win.

I continue to live with my parents, and David continues his seldom visits to his wife and children.

One night I fall asleep but wake again when I hear a small noise coming from my bedroom window. The window faces the street. I am surprised to see David standing in the street. Then I see a small stone on the ground outside.

"David?! What's going on? Did you just throw this stone to the window?"

"Yes. I wanted you to wake up! I am here."

Careful not to wake up the children, I open the door and let him in. He is drunk but determined to play the role of a husband. In the morning he leaves. I do not hear from him again, until sometime later he shows up again late at night.

Many times this act continues. In the mornings he leaves, and I do not hear from him again until the next time he shows up. Eventually I start feeling bad about this. Many times David is drunk.

I am physically exhausted and intellectually drained from the up and downs in my personal relationship and Georgia's collapsed economical life. I long to break out of this environment. I want to jump out of this endless circle and make a change.

My mom feels my pain and supports me every way she can. One day she hands me a newspaper ad.

A newly established cable company, Ayeti-TV, is offering modern technology to its future customers instead of the antennas everyone has always used. The company is looking for marketing representatives who will deliver its message about the benefits of cable TV to potential customers.

I stare at the ad. These kinds of positions are completely new for our mentality. Marketing and sales were undeveloped fields during the Soviet system. If advanced thinkers and business-minded people revealed themselves during the Communism Era, they would be horribly punished for their visions and smartness, because free-thinkers were a danger to the mind-controlling communist system. Success was perceived as "government crime." Everyone was aware of the unfairness, but no one could show open protest against the government. Such people were sentenced to years in prison. And this was not during the Stalin years. This was in the 1970s.

But now here is a job opportunity that will pay forward-thinkers. I am ready for new steps. I decide to try this opportunity.

I will not mind my exhaustion. After all, what other choice do we all have except to be brave and try to walk on unfamiliar paths?

※

In the morning I get dressed and sneak out from the house, as the boys would beg and cry not to let me go. The small-sized apartments naturally make us get closer and attached. We are always a close part of each other's lives. The boys love their grandparents, but they have a difficult time to let one of us go from their sight, because of that attachment.

I get on bus N 27 and ride for forty minutes to the destination. These forty minutes are peaceful minutes, which I have been deprived of for so long.

When I arrive, I feel excited to apply for the job of salesperson. The cable TV company has rented a small apartment for its office. The front room I enter, and the others I can see, are lit with low-voltage light bulbs. These use less electricity, and this way the company pays less money for the electric bill.

"Hello, I would like to work here," I say. A receptionist directs me down a very small hall. I go to the doorway of a little bigger room, which previously was a family room or bedroom. Through a haze of cigarette smoke and people coming and going, I see people busy at three old desks and several others seated on old wooden chairs and a couch.

The desk nearest to me has an ashtray on it full of ashes. In the room, many people's fingers and mouths hold cigarettes. Everyone smokes their sorrows away, one cigarette after another.

"I would like to work here," I tell the man at the desk.

He points me to another room, where the manager sits.

As I enter, the manager stands up and shakes my hand with a welcoming face. "Hello! Please have a seat. How did you hear about us?"

I sit across the desk from him. "From the newspaper ad."

"Are you willing to work as a salesperson?"

I can make some money, I think, not knowing much about what a salesperson job exactly means.

"Yes," I answer, outwardly confident and strong. I desperately need to help support my family, and I need breaks from being mother to three small boys 24/7.

The manager observes the determination I show. Then he grants me the job.

Excitement shakes my body.

༄

The bus rides to work and to visit potential customers are highlights in my exhausting and gloomy days. There I sit among a busy and loud crowd, and I am able to lose myself in reading books and healing my tired soul.

David doesn't really know or care about my job, as he spends very little time with me or the boys. My mom is happy for me. She knows how much I have needed breaks from my situation.

To fulfill my job requirements, I visit families and explain the positive sides and new opportunities that cable television can offer. It isn't easy to convince Georgians of new ideas and ways. They have concerns, disbeliefs, and hesitations.

Eventually the skill of communication is uncovered in me and, one after another, subscribers fill the list. That skill is noticed by management also. As soon as one region is covered with cables, they transfer me to a new location.

But the most problematic challenge I face for having accepted the job as a salesperson remains the emotional part. These types of jobs are not counted as prestigious in the Georgian mind-set. The pressure of that viewpoint is even heavier for me because I am the mother of three small children.

"What kind of respectable woman, the mother of three children, would knock on strangers' doors?" I have dreaded to hear that rebuking of society. Afraid to be condemned, I haven't dared to tell my management or coworkers that I have children.

This softly killing judgment is making painful holes in my soul. Part of me doesn't care about others' approval, but the other part is still tormented by stereotypes. These people are the same way—gripped by labels.

As the job gets busier, I am expected to spend extra time and stay overtime at work. It becomes hard to keep the secret. I have to tell the truth, even if I lose the job.

One day I knock on the manager's door. "I would like to say something."

"Yes, Maka."

"I can't work extra hours."

"Why? Aren't you happy to have a job and make extra money?"

"Yes, but I have three small boys at home, and they aren't easy for my parents to handle for so many hours."

A long silence follows my revelation.

All my previous fear lifts. I am not scared anymore. On the contrary, I feel as strong as never before since I have started to work.

From that same moment, I am treated with great respect and understanding. The manager and everyone on the team takes my news in positive ways. The rejection I had feared never materializes.

✆

Cold and dark December nights follow. Sixteen-floor apartment buildings with three families on each floor is my target. Many times I walk along dark hallways, because electricity is often out in the whole city. Scared and cold with a flashlight in my hand, I pray to God and keep going.

After each workday, I run as fast as I can to the bus station, eager to catch up on time spent apart from my boys. In that darkness, I hide behind my scarf as I run, and let out my anger toward my husband, blaming him for my sufferings.

But God always sends me signs of hope, and in different ways. One of them comes to me after work one night, through the encouraging words of my friend, Erekle, a project manager, spoken in his strong, baritone voice. "One day the spring will come, and the trees will bloom in our streets too."

In these words, and in that voice, is the power that I need to continue forward. As weeks and months pass into warm weather, he says the words to me again when I need to hear them. They help me to overcome. Many times tears hit me, but I try hard to stop them and never let anyone to see them. I just keep going on.

Maybe all of these troubles are the tests that life gives us. To pass or to fail them defines where our future roads will take us.

※

Chaos reigns everywhere in Tbilisi. It is August of 1998, and Levan is four years old.

One morning my mom says, "Maka, let's take boys and visit your Grandma Jathu. That will make her happy, and also the boys will get away from city's hot air."

My energetic boys love the outdoors. This will give them the chance to run around freely, loosing the energy they cannot loose inside our small condo. We decide to go.

Grandma Jathu's village is about seven hours' drive from the city. As we approach, the minivan rolls slowly over the narrow, unpaved road. Its wheels jump in holes, and we do too with them. On both sides of the road, fences are built with stones and cement, each fence different from the next. Gates are made of metal, and inside them are huge front yards that stretch back to big two-floor houses covered in green moss.

"Boys, we are almost here," I joyfully exclaim as I see Grandma Jathu's gate. Her house is built from bricks and cement, the technique used in the west part of Georgia for building houses.

Mom parks the car, and we all step out. A tall woman is feeding a few chickens. "Grandma! We are here!" I call to her.

"Oh, my dears!" She drops the chicken feed she is holding and rushes toward us. "The boys are here! I am so happy to see you!"

We hug each other beside the van, and then all of us enter through the gate.

Grandma's two acres of green, grassy yard hasn't changed since I was a child. The leafy hundred-year-old oak tree still stands, giving shade and character to the yard. Next to the house is the well of fresh and delicious water, ready to cool you down no matter how hot the day is.

Beyond the house, two acres of corn fields merge with rows of nut and fruit trees. As children, my brother and I climbed the cherry trees and ate healthy and delightful fruit right from their branches.

Memories of my childhood fill my thoughts. I close my eyes and see scenes from when we came to visit Grandma when my brother and I were children.

"I will catch a chicken, and we will soon have dinner!" Grandma says and then runs after the chickens. My brother, Levan, and I are so excited to see her running to try to catch a chicken. Surprisingly, she always gets one really quick.

"Grandma! You are a professional at catching chickens!" I laugh from happiness.

She disappears into the kitchen. Before long, Levan and I hear our mom calling, "Dinner is ready!"

In the middle of the dining room sits a big rectangular walnut table. On its sides and ends, old style chairs have small, round ornaments on their back posts. The table is set with Georgian traditional dishes: chicken in walnut sauce; corn bread; Tkemali, the inseparable sauce to a Georgian feast; homemade cheese; and fresh milk from the neighbor's cow.

I open my eyes again. Now, after so many years, conditions are completely different in the villages. Like her neighbors, Grandma can't afford to have many chickens and no longer has pigs. Her house seems to be falling apart. The yard could use some work. Still, we are happy just to be together.

Dinner time is approaching. "We are going to have spaghetti tonight," Grandma says. "Maka, why don't you feed the boys some of these chicken nuggets, and when our spaghetti dinner is ready, we can enjoy ourselves, talk, and remember treasured moments from the past."

Relieved that the boys have a big, open yard to play in, I feel some freedom. I feed them chicken nuggets. "Now you can play in the yard nicely." I watch them start toward the door, then I turn around to help with dinner.

Behind me, a large pot of spaghetti is boiling on a primitively made electric stove that is only knee tall.

"Now we can have a peaceful evening." I take a deep breath.

In a second, I hear laughing and the sound of small feet running past the stove. My head turns toward the sound. Levan trips on the cord of the stove and falls onto his back, knocking the pot over toward him. Boiling water and pasta spill over his chest.

A horrified scream breaks from me. Instinctively I jump and pick up my little boy. "Help!!!" My voice carries out to the village.

My mom and Grandma Jathu run to us. "Water, cold water." Someone is trying to pour water on my son.

Poor Levan cries, but nothing and no one can save him from the misery. It is already done.

In minutes, the house is filled with neighbors. "We need to take him to the emergency," someone says who has their wits with them.

A man runs home and comes back with his car. Emergency vehicles and phone services are like a lost dream in the villages.

With neighbors' help, we manage to put Levan into the car and drive to the hospital. The only hospital and emergency room in the whole area is a half hour drive away. Unfortunately, none of us expects it will be equipped on a professional level, especially to treat a burnt child. I shake as I think, *What will happen to Levan?*

By the time we reach the hospital, it is about nine at night. I waste no time carrying Levan inside.

"We need the doctor, as soon as possible!" My demand awakens the dormant walls of the hospital building. Several pairs of eyes turn in our direction, but it seems no one comes for a long time, as if the nurses have been sleeping from boredom.

"What is going on?" Slowly a woman gets up from her chair.

"We need the doctor! Hurry up!" I urge her.

"We will call the doctor. Can you wait please?"

It seems they don't realize how serious Levan's condition is, or how crucial time is now.

The man who drove us here looks at me. "We need to drive to Tbilisi!" he says firmly. "I don't think they can provide enough help here."

Mom and I agree.

"Hurry up." He waves us toward the door. "Let's get in the car—"

"We need to pick up the twins!" Though I'm in shock, I still remember that I have to take Sandro and Nika with me.

The minivan is big enough to fit us all. We drive in the middle of the night. The streets look dark and lonely, but the twins sleep calmly. I hold dear Levan's hand. His bravery makes me want to be stronger. He looks into my eyes and gives me hope that everything will be okay.

I am crying inside, but trying not to show him my weakness.

"Mommy, are Sandro and Nika okay?" he asks me with his caring voice.

"Yes, they are good, Levan." I feel astonished that he can think of his brothers in this difficult time.

After seven hours of driving, around seven in the morning, we reach the city. I have become more scared and confused with each hour that has passed. I can't think very clearly because of my fear.

"Let's go home," I say to my mother. "I need to call David and tell him about the accident."

At home, I call David at his parents' house and tell him about the accident.

"I am coming right now," he says.

About thirty minutes later, he arrives.

During the wait, my thoughts have cleared. "We need to take him to hospital," I tell David.

"Hold on. My friend knows someone who can cure burns with some homemade medicine. Definitely the hospital would cost a lot. Maybe we can avoid that." David leaves again. Another hour goes by before David comes back with creams and bandages.

"Hurry up, Maka," he says. "We need to put this on Levan's body."

As we do, Levan screams, cries, and begs us for someone else to help.

We keep trying to help. Soon he calms down and seems sleepy.

In the middle of a hot Georgian August, people usually go away on vacation, so this day the city is empty. But God is definitely watching out for Levan. Unexpectedly, our second-floor neighbor, George, whose wife, Marina, is a pediatrician, enters the building.

"Hi, Maka. What are you doing here? Aren't you supposed to be on a vacation?"

"Oh, Givi, Levan had an accident. He's burnt!"

Only a minute or two later, Dr. Marina comes down to see Levan's condition. Her expression tells us that what she sees is unimaginable.

"What are you guys doing at home? Have you completely lost your minds?! Right away, you need to take this little boy to the hospital! I demand!"

By the order in her voice, I know things are very serious.

David goes to the telephone and calls an ambulance. Soon all of us are racing to the hospital behind the speeding vehicle. Screaming sirens cut my heart, but I can barely feel anything anymore.

Our car stops right in front of the emergency entrance. With quick moves, three men in uniform take out the stretcher and roll my already weakened boy inside through the doors of the ER. I follow inside up to the doors.

"Ma'am, you have to wait here. They will take care of him. Your son is in good hands!"

A kind woman in registration calms me down, and I sit on a chair. What other choice do I have?

After thirty minutes, the doctor comes out. "Crucial time has been lost," he tells us. "But we will do everything possible. In burning accidents, time is very important. Unfortunately, you brought your son to the hospital more than twenty-four hours after the accident happened. The more time that is lost, the deeper the damage will go into the skin."

My body trembles as I hear this.

The doctor adds, "The second bad thing that can happen in burning accidents is the size of the damaged part. And unfortunately, one-third of your son's body is burned. And the third very bad thing that could happen is an infection. Sadly, Levan's wound is infected too."

All I can think is, *If only I had known more about burning complications! I would not even hesitate but would have come straight to the hospital!*

That evening, exhausted from emotions, I arrive home, go to the second floor, and ring the bell. Givi, Dr. Marina's husband, opens the door.

Immediately he asks, "How is Levan? What's going on?"

"They put him into intensive care. Givi, I would like to thank you and Marina for your attention and care. You both saved my son!" Without any words left, I go downstairs.

My mom and I sit together. We are all exhausted. None of us has words left to talk. There is one main thing we need to worry now—money. I pick up the phone and dial my brother.

"Can I speak with Levan, please?" I nervously try to speak in English to a stranger on the other end of the line. My brother is working on his master's degree in political science at the Columbus, Ohio, university.

"Just a moment." The woman's soft voice is a little calming. I need that effect just now.

"Hello! How are you guys?" The peaceful voice of my brother does not fit my alarmed condition.

"Levan, we have a little problem here." I want to slowly prepare him for the shocking news. "Levaniko was burned in an accident, and he is in intensive care. We need money for treatments. It is very expensive to treat burns, and we have no money here, you know."

"What? How? When?" Levan is anxious to hear all the details about the accident.

By the end of the day, one thousand American dollars has been transferred from my brother's account to mine.

Days and weeks pass. Many more one thousand dollars are needed for treatments. David sells his parents' apartment to pay the debts.

We go through one month of hell in the ICU. I stay at the hospital where I endure sleepless nights and scared days. For a month I do not see my twins. My parents and David are taking care of them, as well as visiting us in the hospital, bringing food and medicines.

After one month Levan is released from the hospital, but changing bandages, medicines, nurses, injections, and Levan's crying still continue, as autumn and then winter passes.

Once a month we go to a ten-day treatment at the doctor's house-clinic. Levan, this five-year-old boy who has gone through so much agony, is still so understanding of our circumstances. We cannot afford to take a cab, so we have to walk, even with Levan's painful burns, to the doctor's house.

And so we do. The route becomes familiar to us. We walk down the slope for about twenty minutes. Then we turn left and go down a small hill. Soon the gate appears, and there Levan's and my trepidation begins.

"Levan you are a strong boy! You can do this, right?" I try to encourage him, but in my heart I know what a painful experience he has to keep going through.

The waiting room is always full of patients, mostly children. Hearing horrible stories from other moms is even more heartbreaking. We often wait for thirty to forty minutes. This is a time of suffering. I want to protect my son from hearing children cry from the other room. I want to mute that room, but I am unable to do so. All I can do is to sit, hold my strong little boy's hand, and squeeze it to let him know that we are strong together and that no matter the pain we can overcome this experience.

When we are called into that other room, the medical instrument with a shotgun shape, which shoots Levan's burns with a drug, is equal to a pistol bullet. These sessions to reduce scarring are reducing our joy as well!

Ultimately, regardless of miserable conditions or the lack of modern technology and medications, the Georgian doctors still manage to treat the burns. But many scars are left.

The scars on Levan's body are like the scars on the souls of Georgian people. Just like burning starts and finds its way deeper into the skin, turning into the permanent scars on it, political changes—which started as the collapsing of communism and which we thought was the way to freedom—slowly starts making cracks on our souls, continuing painfully deeper and deeper, leaving permanent scars on souls.

Alarmed with his nephew's condition, but with a hope to find a way for the scars to disappear, Uncle Levan contacts the Children's Burn Institute at the Shriners' Hospital for Children in Cincinnati for possible support.

I read my brother's e-mail to discover what he has learned. "Maka, four large hospitals here, including one in Cincinnati, treat burnt children. Philanthropists and benevolent people from this organization cure injured children from all over the world without cost. Sister organizations cover travel costs or reach out to others to find a place for newcomers to stay." Levan explains how we might receive their help for my little son.

After I answer his e-mail, Levan contacts hospital officials and explains the situation. They offer to help us.

Levan and I start to prepare the documents. This process takes six months. Then, one year after the date of the accident, we make arrangements for the journey for medical reasons to the New World, the United States of America!

Miraculously everything gets taken care of. A divine couple, Mr. and Mrs. Paroz, volunteer to shelter us at their home for a possible six- to eighteen-month stay.

Levan and I will soon step into a completely unknown and unfamiliar experience. This is a pretty brave decision for me. I will have to leave my active three-year-old twins to my parents and husband, who is somewhat lost in uncertainty.

But suddenly a whole new possibility and the light of hope shines on the horizon. Regardless of the unpleasant reason for going and that I will not see my two littlest boys for so very long, I can feel this travel will be a break from the whirl of politics, a shattered economy, unprotected social conditions, and my challenging marriage.

The unknown journey to come is somehow filling me with hope.

Even so, the night we are to leave, I feel the pressure of all that is to come. The traveling route includes changing four planes and five airports. We will fly from Tbilisi, Georgia, to Kiev, Ukraine. Then on to Budapest, Hungary. That new plane will carry us over an entire ocean to New York, USA. After New York, we will fly to Cincinnati, Ohio, our final destination.

And before we travel, I have to say good-bye to my parents and my twins for a possible eighteen months. It is very painful to get used to this idea.

"Levaniko, my dear, listen to me. Tonight we will go to the airport. Sandro and Nika will be sleeping, but we are not going to wake them up. We will sneak out quietly from the house. If they wake up and see us leaving, they'll cry. Tomorrow morning Grandma will take them to the park, Grandpa will tell jokes to them, and they will be fine. Don't worry, everything will be okay!"

When the time comes to leave, I take Levan's hand and hug my mom and dad. "We will be fine," I assure them. "Take care of yourselves and the twins." Then we sneak out from the house, leaving behind my sleeping boys, parents toughened from sorrows, and my heart.

David is waiting outside to drive us to the airport.

I am strong, and everything will be okay, I repeat in my mind, maybe encouraging myself most of all. As we put our suitcases into the car and get in, I avoid looking at our home. In fact, I block the thought of my golden, curly-haired boys waking up tomorrow morning and searching for their mommy; and of them at night waiting for her to sing them a lullaby and put them to sleep. That will not be the reality for a long, long time.

And so we drive away.

I don't like to show my emotions and tears to others, and especially in the difficult moment leaving my parents who are already heartbroken and full of sorrow. I wear a mask of calm and strength.

Beneath that mask, I am a young and frightened mother of three boys, tired from raising them in unreasonable conditions, a troubled marriage, and the disordered state of the country's relations. At the age of twenty-nine, life has tested me with plentiful problems to handle and solve. And now I am going to an unknown, unfamiliar world. Having a very heavy burden on my shoulders, but with no other way out, I have to carry it on.

I have to lead the road.

Chapter Seven
Foreign Country

Cincinnati, Ohio, United States of America
October 1999

The long and exhausting travel is over. After many new images, aircrafts, and airports, we land in Cincinnati.

My heart beats fast from excitement. I leave the plane, holding tightly to my son's hand, and search for our hosts among all the people. Suddenly I see a big white paper waving in the air:

LEVAN & MAKA
WELCOME TO AMERICA

A thin, elegant lady with snowy white hair and a gentle smile waves at us. Next to her stands a man about five feet nine inches tall.

They must be our hosts, I tell myself and walk toward them.

The man greets us. "Hello, Maka. How are you? You are finally here, in America!" The man is a representative from the charitable organization. He introduces himself and his lovely wife as Mr. and Mrs. Paroz.

Mrs. Paroz turns to Levan and hands a fluffy brown bear to him. "Hello, Levan. Welcome to America! This little bear is for you. He wants to say hi to you too!"

Levaniko's face lights up. He takes the bear and hugs it right away in his arms. Love and care fill my five-year-old's heart who, after all, isn't quite sure where he really is, who doesn't quite understand what "foreign country" really means, or foreign people, or foreign language.

As we walk, I try to stay focused on Mr. and Mrs. Paroz's conversation with me. I tense my attention, trying to catch the words and get the questions. I had thought I had known some English, but suddenly all my hopes collapse. I barely can say a word or understand what they are trying to tell me.

Fear starts to overpower me, but this amazing lady very diplomatically starts using gestures to help me understand. She speaks very slow and clear. Courage returns to me, and soon so do words and phrases.

We pick up our suitcases, and then Mr. Paroz leads us outside to their brown, leather-seated car. Levan and I get comfortable in the backseat. My little boy's face is all in smiles. He has never before sat in this kind of "cool" car.

"Please, put your seatbelts on," Mrs. Paroz turns back with smile and asks us.

"To do what?" I hear the words because she spells them slowly, but I have no idea what she is talking about.

"Seatbelts." She lifts an odd device that crosses over her and shows us what to do.

"Seatbelts." I try the new word. "What do you mean?" I still do not understand, though I see one next to me and another by Levan. I don't know where such belts came from and what they are for. They seem to be attached to the car, but I never saw them before. I never saw one in cars in Georgia.

Mr. Paroz opens our doors and helps us to click our seatbelts into their places. "This is for security," he says with a smile, but I can feel his firm character. I see there will be some rules we do not know but will have to learn.

"No one is using them in Georgia," I mumble. As I do, I realize a way in which Georgians differ from the people in America. Georgians don't like rules and try to ignore them.

While we drive, I look around the vehicle. "What is the name of this car?" I ask out of interest.

"Chev-ro-let." Kind Mrs. Paroz spells this for us.

The word sounds so French and so musical. Levan likes its strange sound too. As we continue toward their home, he sings, "Chev-ro-let, Chev-ro-let." He is happy.

I am happy too. The car is riding smoothly on quiet, beautiful streets. I have never seen anything like them before.

With classical music on the radio, and with so much excitement, so many new things, people, words, and ideas, so much happiness even, I become drowsy from travel. My eyes close, my brain sinks into the classical music, and I fall to sleep.

"We are here."

I hear the words. Slowly I try to open my eyes and come out from drowsiness and sleep. Objects start to come into focus. Beyond the window I see a long road going up a hill, and evergreen trees are everywhere. The car rolls up the hill and stops right in front of a big, beautiful house that is surrounded with amazingly beautiful flowers.

This is a huge house?! Where are we? Inquisitive thoughts enter my mind. *We are supposed to stay at their home, but this place looks like a sanatorium?*

Confused, and lost in time zone changes and jet lag, I try to divide reality from unreality. It all seems surreal. Nothing looks familiar. I've seen these kinds of picture-perfect houses in American movies, but that was in movies, right? Movies means this should not be real. Even a sanatorium could not be this big or beautiful.

Suddenly I realize that such thoughts full of disbelief must be soviet thinking. "Where are we?" Dying from curiosity, I dare to ask.

"This is our house," Mrs. Paroz tells us. "This is where you guys will live now."

"Well." No other words come to me. I get out of the car. It still feels unrealistic that this house could belong to one family, and even more, that we are supposed to live here. A small path leads to the door, and flowers follow it along both sides. Next to the path is a short, small tree with a birdhouse.

Mrs. Paroz leads us to the large front door with a welcoming smile. "I will show you the house and your rooms. And please call me Mama Paroz."

Suddenly the wall between us becomes softer, and we become closer. I feel loved and respected, acknowledged and appreciated. In my country feelings like these are lost in the past. And now that past and my own country also seem surreal.

Inside, the hallway room is full of light and plants. Until now I have never been in a house with glass walls. This room has them on two sides. On the third, in a corner, is a mirror with an antique carved frame and an old-style armchair, waiting for a guest to come and rest in peacefulness. The plants have huge leaves. The room reminds me a rainforest, which I have seen in movies.

Farther on, another room cozy with couches and a fireplace invite us into more peacefulness. Firewood sits right next to the bricks, promising that a fire could flame at any time. On the mantel are picture frames with beautiful people's photographs in them.

Family. Peace. Happiness. Togetherness. The words surface in my mind. I swallow pain. My boys, my family, where are they?

"Let's go, guys." Mrs. Paroz's sweet voice wakes me from my thoughts. "I will show you downstairs, your rooms."

Hearing her kindness, a happy smile comes to my face. I hold my hand out to Levan, and we follow her downstairs. He acts so mature all the time?!

Our feet fall softly into carpet. Everything, and even this, is unusual for me. In my country everyone has hardwood floors. Carpets are a decoration, and they are mostly handmade Oriental style rugs with picturesque designs and patterns. Here the carpet is just plain, but fluffy. *Well, something different*, I think.

A basement is also a completely new thing. In our basements, or more like storages, we keep canned food and jars for winter, and old, unneeded things. But here, this is a room with furniture, a corner with toys and books for entertaining children, a fireplace, pillows, and blankets—and bedrooms.

"This room is for you, Maka."

Mrs. Paroz opens a wooden door, and I see a beautifully decorated room. Floral print sheets steal my vision. The blanket with green leaves and light pink flowers seems so warm and soft. *I could be lost in sleep in here*, I think.

"This is Levan's room."

I am quickly awakened from my dreaminess. *What? Levan's room? Are they going to give us two separate rooms? What? We've never had separate rooms before?!* In our condo we have two bedrooms. One is for my parents, and the other is for my boys and me. And now they are giving me a separate room to stay in?

My consciousness feels lost and confused. I definitely need time to digest so many new things, and so many differences.

Levan is happy to have his own bed. He has always shared not only one room but one bed with his brothers.

The United States is certainly a foreign country.

✑

The virtuous, gentle woman, Mrs. Paroz, cares like a grandmother for Levan, and like a mother for me. "Call me Mama Paroz," she encourages me again on our second day, and so they become Mama and Papa Paroz.

Our third day in their home, their son, Pierre, and his five-year-old son, Andrew, come to visit and get to know Levan. Andrew has brought his bicycle to share with Levan during the visit. These kind people welcome us as if we are part of their family.

Two days later, it is time to go to an appointment at Shriners Hospital.

"We are leaving!" Mrs. Paroz picks up the car keys.

"Chev-ro-let! Chev-ro-let," Levan starts to sing happily. In the car, he doesn't need a reminder about seatbelts. He is happy to click his and mine in place.

We drive. Curvy roads lost in forest continue into a small town. We drive through the town to a highway, and finally we get to a huge hospital building.

In our understanding a hospital is a white, cold, and scary building, where not only children but adults also hate to go. But here, suddenly, we discover ourselves in a totally different atmosphere. The place overflows with the most beautiful flowers. We see fountains, and we see children's playgrounds decorated with colorful toys.

Inside, the hospital staff smiles to everyone they pass on the way to their destinations. They wear uniforms with Mickey Mouses, bears, and flowers printed on them.

"Welcome to our hospital!" The representative has been expecting us. She gives us a welcoming smile and leads us along a hallway. The corridors are as colorful and fun as the rest of the place.

It is impossible for Levan to realize that he is surrounded by doctors. Everyone smiles here, and everything looks wonderful and exciting.

Their smiles pour warmth and kindness into my heart, filling me with hope that, somewhere, happiness still exists. These smiles immediately melt the fear, cold, and fatigue in me, and for the first time in many years, a total peace comes into my heart.

I remember that this "American smile" has been a subject of ridicule in Georgia. "Why do they smile all the time?" Georgians often ask when conversations turn to the United States. But maybe countries of the former Soviet Union have difficulty understanding the power of this smile. One should probably feel it.

We reach a room where we wait for the doctor. Soon we hear a knock on the door, and the doctor walks in.

"Hello! So here you are, Levan!" He greets him warmly and cheerfully.

Levan smiles back at him. Never before have I watched a doctor greet a patient with respect and humbleness, not to mention a child patient. His greeting breaks through any difference in age and profession.

The doctor explores Levan's scars. "Seems like Georgian doctors have done a great job. Because of late treatment, scars are left, but the wounds have healed. At this stage, we can't do much. Some massage sessions, creams, and materials to go, and you are free to return to Georgia!" He is happy to announce his conclusion to us.

This news should fill me with joy that we can go back home and be with the twins. But the opposite happens! Everything is more like a shock than happy emotions. I have become accustomed to the idea that it will be several months that I will be away from my boys. I have used so much energy to adapt the idea of not seeing my twins for a long time, and now, a few weeks will pass, and then we will be free to go?!

What about Levan? Will massage sessions and creams really help him much? Is there nothing more they can do for him?

※

When we are not at the hospital with Leven, the Paroz family makes sure we see some American culture. Pierre and his family take us to a children's museum, and for the first time in my life I see a 3D film on a half-round screen! The ocean seems to splash on my face, and I ride in the fastest train.

One day Mama and Papa Paroz's children and grandchildren come to visit at the house. Everyone wants to get to know us. "Grandma" Paroz cooks Swiss fondue—delicious melted cheese—and makes a salad from fresh leaves that she has picked from her own garden.

After dinner she places small portions into containers for everyone to take home. As she does this, I remember my own grandmother. She would always cook delicious Georgian food, and then she would put extra into containers for us to take home.

I think more about my grandma. Because of traditions, and partially because of our small living spaces, most of the time three generations live together in apartments. The good outcome from this is close relationships with each other. We are always surrounded with love, attention, and care. And there is always wisdom that the old generation shares. We are able to hear their stories, memories, proverbs, and the history of our country's brave past. These enrich our imaginations, knowledge, and grow our roots and love for our land stronger and stronger.

Our days in the United State are full of cultural similarities and differences. Some differences cause us to feel confused.

On a day that Levan and I go for a walk, we come to a street crossing. A big stop sign lets us know to stop. A car approaches the intersection and also stops. We stand and wait. The driver politely waves his hand. I don't know what to do. The driver waves again.

"Okay, Levan, I guess we can cross the street," I tell my son. We start to cross, and this polite man lets us before he drives on. My curiosity does not calm down. As soon we arrive home, I tell the incident to Mama Paroz.

"Maka, in this country pedestrians have a right to go first. Cars give the way to people. So not only was this man nice, but also the law tells him to do so."

I feel relief. But this behavior seems so foreign! I tell Mama Paroz, "No one in Georgia would let you cross the street in front of them. They would drive on you if you tried!"

Many other differences are also foreign to us. We cannot become accustomed to big houses or beautifully mowed green lawns, or to skyscrapers and people of many nations. Or to smiles on people's faces. Casual smiling is not something that Georgians are familiar with.

One day I show Mama Paroz the photo album I brought along of my family. "Maka, I am looking at these pictures in your album, and your dad never smiles in any of them. Why is that?" She cannot hide her astonishment, and I am completely shocked to realize that she is correct.

My dad never smiles in pictures? Really? A brainstorm starts. I try to distinguish reasons, and then come to a conclusion. Our history, problems, worries, and sorrows make smiling harder to express. My dad's personal story, unfortunately, is deeply connected with the Communist Party's horrible actions. Our life experiences, based on a geopolitical situation, have never given us a chance to stop worrying. All of these experiences limit the expression of smiles.

Papa Paroz sits near us. His heavy French accent tells me he was not born in America, but still he smiles often. I ask, "Papa Paroz, when and how did you come to this country?"

"I came to America from the Swiss Alps as a nineteen-year-old boy. I did not speak a word of English. It was a time of economic development, and I knew Swiss machines would make a difference. I learned the language, used opportunities wisely, and at the same time strengthened connections with my homeland."

Switzerland's high-quality machinery can make any detailed part, starting with the tiniest gear for watches, and engines. Papa Paroz brought these machines to America.

"It was not easy to start the business. At first I hired only twenty people. We produced necessary mechanisms and looked for clients who would be interested in our products." Soon the number of hired workers began to increase. Today two hundred people are employed in the company.

Again, I realize how this way of thinking is so foreign to the way we think in Georgia. For seventy years communists killed men in Georgia and in other soviet countries for having ideas like these. Because of this, we do not know how to think in this way.

If Georgian people could learn this, things might actually get better for my country.

∅

After Levaniko's treatments are finished and we say good-bye to the children's hospital, Papa Paroz buys tickets for us to visit my brother for one month. Levan has recently moved to Minneapolis. After one month we will come back to Cincinnati and then return to Georgia.

The day we will go to Minneapolis, I wake up early in the chilly morning. "Levan, wake up. We are going to see Uncle Levan. Finally, you will meet with him in person. This is going to be a big and happy trip for us!"

Right away my little boy jumps from the bed and starts to get ready. My favorite breakfast is already on the table as usual. We eat quickly and run outside. Papa Paroz is in car. His Swiss punctuality is always noticeable.

At the bus station, he gives me a hundred-dollar bill. "Have this for the road," he says.

We thank him and tell him good-bye.

Greyhound buses are lined up to take passengers between the states. People with various appearances, colors, and outfits move around the station. Then I see our bus. "Chicago" the sign says. During our fifteen-hour ride, we will stop in Chicago and switch to a different bus.

Approaching Chicago from the southern side is a breathtaking experience. Skyscrapers with inimitable views suddenly appear with magical powers to embolden and inspire you, whoever you are—even just a traveler passing by. No matter who you are, this view will leave its unforgettable imprint.

We switch buses late in the day, and the night view in this majestic city is even more powerful. A million lights lighting the darkness almost reach the sky. I am out of breath.

Levan and I fall asleep, even though it is impossible to sleep well on these chairs. A little while later, a boy from Mississippi wakes me up to let me know that we have arrived in Saint Paul, Minnesota. It is four in the morning.

The bus has arrived thirty minutes earlier than the supposed time. We will have to wait for my brother. Immediately I wake up Levan. The bus has stopped, and only a few passengers get out. We do also.

I hope we won't freeze, I think. It's dark and cold here. The streets are empty since the city is sleeping. I look around but do not see my brother anywhere. The bus drives away.

Levan cannot wait to meet with his uncle who has his name. They have never seen each other before.

We wait only two minutes before I see my brother walking to us. "Levan! Oh my God! We have not seen each other for eight years!" We hug each other. It seems to me he has not changed at all, and even like these eight years have not been absent.

"Levaniko, how are you?" Uncle Levan greets his nephew in our native language, as Levaniko only speaks Georgian. My brother's Georgian language is as perfect as it's always been. His linguistic talent enables him to speak three languages as if born to each of them.

Levaniko becomes shy, but he has the manners characteristic of his age and answers politely. "I'm well."

In Levan's car I see that Minneapolis is beautifully illuminated at night. My brother and I talk and share stories like we always have.

Suddenly I feel strange. So many years of separation, but it seems like yesterday that he left home, as if he has never gone anywhere. We have continued right from where we left off. I have a smile on my face full of happiness and satisfaction.

Soon we reach a two-story apartment building with brown brick. Levan opens the door to the building. We enter a narrow hallway, and steps covered with carpet lead upstairs.

"Janet is sleeping," Levan cautions us, "so let's go quietly inside so we do not wake her up. Our apartment is on the second floor."

Levaniko is excited and runs up the stairs to the second floor.

Levan opens the door to his apartment. "This is our home."

Levaniko and I are delighted to look around. To my surprise there are no table or chairs in the kitchen, or anywhere else.

"Levan, how do you guys eat? You have no table." I am confused.

"On the couch." His reply is very short.

On the couch? What does "on the couch" mean? I wonder.

We meet his wife, Janet, when she wakes up. She has long, curly blonde hair and greets us warmly.

She bakes muffins and makes coffee. There is a delicious smell around.

"Coffee is ready," Janet says. "Let's enjoy some."

I go to the kitchen, pour some coffee, and . . .

"Levan? Where are we going to sit?"

"We sit on the couch and have dinner in that room," he tells me.

I look into the room and see only one couch and one armchair.

"So, what kind of life is this? A kitchen without table and chairs?!" My brain starts thinking of how to improve the situation.

That evening Levan takes us to visit their friends near the twin cities of Minneapolis and Saint Paul. Nodar and Eka are emigrants from Georgia too. They have been living in Minneapolis for several years. Nodar is an artist. He designs smoking pipes from metal. They have begun to attract great interest from American designers. Eka, his wife, is a manager.

Their small studio apartment feels cozy, and its walls are filled with paintings. Eka serves us tea and cakes. We talk about

Georgia, surrounded by the art of our culture. We feel connected immediately.

On the way home, I see many new things, but having no chairs in the kitchen still bothers me.

We visit our friends often. One evening while we drive home from seeing them, I notice some chairs put out in the street.

"What are these chairs? Why are they in the street?" I ask Levan in surprise.

"Americans often do this," he explains. "When they do not need something any longer, they put it out in the street. If somebody needs it, they may take it home. There are some garage sales as well, where you can buy secondhand clothes and furniture."

Though this is a foreign idea, already I know what to do. "Levan, stop the car. We should take these chairs for your kitchen."

Levan does not argue with me. In a few minutes, we are driving home with four chairs. Levaniko is delighted with the new furniture.

A kitchen should have chairs.

※

In the days that follow, we purchase an armchair, a TV table, and several other furnishings for Janet and Levan's apartment. Now they can freely invite guests.

One evening everyone is at home. I hear somebody knocking at the door. Janet walks over and opens it partially. She talks with someone on the other side of the half-opened door.

"Maka," she calls to me, "my mom sends you her greetings."

Janet's mother? I think, and move toward the door. "Janet, is your mother here? Why are you talking to her by the half-closed door? Why is not she coming in?"

Georgian hospitality wins out. To us, a guest is a gift from God, and according to Georgian tradition, the door is open for guests at any time.

"Hello!" I greet Janet's mother. "You are welcome!" I invite her in, and she is happy that she is invited into the apartment.

For an hour we talk about Georgia and Levaniko. We look at photos, I serve her tea and cake, and she leaves very pleased.

"Visit us again!" I call to her warmly while she goes down the stairs.

We are in America, but still we love our Georgian traditions.

༄

Uncle Levan takes us to the well-known Mall of America. Levaniko enjoys riding on roller coasters and carousels. He has never experienced these before.

After spending one month in Minneapolis, we say good-bye to our hosts, Levan and Janet, and return on the bus to Cincinnati. Soon we say good-bye to the Parozes too.

The morning is emotional and scary. Different feelings hit me, leaving me powerless. I think of Georgia's unrest, and the uncertain situation of my private life. *What is going to happen next? How I am going to continue?*

Pierre comes over to say good-bye. Levaniko is sad to leave his newly gained friend, Andrew. After they leave, Mama Paroz gently hands me an envelope. "Maka, this is from Pierre. He wants you not to worry for some time. Take it."

I take the envelope with modesty. Then I slowly open it. "Oh, dear God! What is this?" I start to mumble. "He left me money? What should I do now?" The gift inside, I would never have dreamed of it in a million years.

"Don't worry, Maka. This money will help you to take care of your boys for some time. You will figure out what best to do with it." Mama Paroz sounds confident.

Her confidence helps my scattered thoughts to gather again. There is one thousand dollars in the envelope. After more uncomfortable feelings and also thoughts of great gratitude, some ideas come to my mind. *I can do so much with this money. I can buy things that my children need—clothing, food, items to improve conditions. . . .*

The list is long, and the money could disappear soon. But the things I've thought of are only short-term improvements. Then I will again be left in a hopeless situation, depending on someone's help.

Suddenly, the sun shines on a cloudy sky. I see the light in the darkness. I will not misuse the money. I do not want that. Somehow I must find a way to use it for greater benefit to my family.

With positive and negative thoughts competing in my head, we drive to the airport. There my healed Levaniko and I leave the kindly Parozes behind us in the country that is so foreign, and also so beautiful.

Chapter Eight
The New Beginning

Tbilisi, Georgia
November 1999

    Living in Tbilisi is not scary anymore. I am seeing the light, and it is an amazing feeling. I know this is not going to be a dead end. New ways will open up in front of me, take me on a bright road, and I will walk safe and strong.

    David still lives at his parents' house. That means my parents and I continue to be the main caretakers of three energetic boys. I have to be brave and take a step forward. I have to provide for my boys.

    After thinking about it for many days, I can no longer keep to myself the idea that has been boiling inside of me. I make an announcement to my parents. "Mom, Dad, instead of spending the money I was given, and still worry afterward where to get more money to live, I have decided to go to America. I will work there and make my own money. This way we don't have to worry about how to take care of the boys and ourselves. And more new roads will open in front of us. I need your support for next six months in taking care of the boys without me."

    It is not an easy offer. It is not an easy decision. It is not easy for my parents to reply.

    My parents!

How much parents do for their children's well-being, their happiness! Many times they swallow their pride to give their children opportunities to go on and test their wings, while at the same time they are praying with their breath for their children's safety. Many times they choose to say nothing in disagreement, even though this hurts so much.

"Maka, how are you going to do all that?" I finally hear Dad's scared voice. He knows I have made up my mind, and there will not be much he can do to change my decision.

"I am already in a tough situation here. If I must be in a tough situation in America to make life a little better for us here, then I will do it."

My family needs me to help provide. And since returning to Georgia, I have felt lost. I feel lost in the uncertainty of life here. I feel lost in my marriage. I must support my family, but I also have to find something. I have to find myself.

When my husband comes to see us and to make his next appearance, I introduce him to my new plan. "David, I've thought a lot. I can't continue like this, with all of this struggle. You are not here physically or materially to help us, so I have decided to buy a ticket to America, work there, and help the situation here to improve. My parents will take care of the boys, and you will come to check on them, right?"

"Okay," David says, suddenly excited with my plan. "Why don't I borrow some money to buy clothes and food for the boys, and when you make money, you send it to me, and I will take care everything." Suddenly he wants to be the person in charge.

"Sorry," I tell David. "I won't be sending money to you. You were not here while my parents and I struggled to take care of the boys in the most difficult moments, when we would walk in freezing weather to doctors' appointments, and worry about money and food. Now I am deciding who I will send money to spend wisely, and that will be my parents. They know exactly what the boys need."

It is very difficult to say good-bye to my children. My heart aches terribly that I have to leave my boys. But I need to support them. And at the same time, I need this trip for my self-search and self-confidence. My marriage is like a big lie, and I cannot continue to live a life of pretend. Lots of women in Georgia live like that, though. By Georgian-traditional opinions, divorce is "vetoed" for women. If I were to stay, I would become a victim of that mentality too. And so would my children.

∅

Six months after Levaniko and I returned to Georgia, with the help of the precious and mighty one thousand United States dollars, I am on my way to America again.

This time the destination is Chicago, and I am traveling alone. It is spring of 2000.

I have learned that Chicago gives many opportunities to emigrants who arrive in search of better futures and fates. This big city is more open-minded to newcomers, making adapting to the new place easier for us. Interacting with people from foreign countries with different cultures and traditions makes its local population more resilient.

Because of this, Chicago, Illinois, is distinguished from other cities and states. For example, in Minneapolis, where my brother lives with his wife, Janet, I would not survive. I have learned about Chicago from my friend Marina's husband, Dato. He lives and works in Chicago.

Georgian friendships have something unique. We are there for each other, no matter the distance, or gender, or place. There is respect, and there is trust. Because of this and the level of friendship I have with Marina, I know Dato will give me the hand to get on my feet.

On the airplane, I think a little of Chicago, but mostly of my sons and home. It seems like I will replace the love of those who are the most important to me with material things, with money itself. Money in exchange for love?!

I must forget the profession I have dreamed of—working in a publishing house—and warm evenings by bonfires enriched with guitars, songs, and lyrics. Forget interacting with interesting people and intellectual endeavors. It is time to survive, to support my family! Besides, I have the aspiration to figure out my place, to find myself in this tangled and scrambled reality of mine.

Below the airplane window, the blue ocean slips away behind us. Now we fly over large pieces of land and giant American cities.

Dear God, give me the ability to be strong. This becomes my prayer, request, and weeping.

∅

Chicago, Illinois, United States
March 2000

While approaching my new home by plane from the east, the pilot makes a huge circle with aquiline playfulness around the Lake Michigan shoreline. We passengers of the huge Boeing aircraft have a greater impression of "Chicagoland." Passengers become enchanted with the city's magnificent sights, the city which at the same time is strong and technocratic, but attractive and the pinnacle of architectural creativity. An army of skyscrapers line up on the coast. Their different shapes and heights in the sky blend in harmony.

The view fills me with admiration and joy. It extends outward over the land an enormous space, and on the east side it is reflected in the water like in a mirror. Such a sight promises you can achieve the impossible. It says that nothing is limited in your thoughts and ideas.

Who knows what takes us far away from home across an ocean? I wonder. *Is it destiny, or is it our character?*

Dato meets me inside the airport. While we wait for my suitcases, he tells me of when he moved to America. Life tested him when a friend, whom he relied on and with whose help he arrived in this foreign country, left him on his own. Despite the lack of proficiency in the English language, Dato soon found a solution. With great willingness he learned the spoken language in a few months, and then he found a job. Now he works as a security guard on the night shift.

I stay with Dato as a guest. During the daytime he has hours free and drives me to agencies so I can find a job.

∞

On famous Milwaukee Street, Lena's agency is well known to many job seekers who want to be in-home caretakers. If she likes us, we are lucky, and she will grant us a job. Otherwise there is no chance.

Her assistant is a rude and annoying man. Everyone hates to see this man, and hates especially to get into his car and go to an interview with a family. His angry character makes everyone feel more miserable then we already are. However, he is "our destiny" at this time. But I never endure his rudeness. One time I even refuse to take the job, and this makes him mad because he loses his share of the money I would have made.

Thankfully I do not have to walk on this road for a long time. In a week Lena sends me to an American family as a nanny.

My responsibility is to take care of three American children. I babysit them from morning until six at night. Afterward I am free, but I have nowhere to go except the basement room where they have given me a place to live. The room without a window!

There I have lots of time to think about my troubled life, and I cry my words into a diary. The notebook papers are no longer flat, because they are often wet from tears. It contains all the anger toward my husband and fears about my uncertain future.

I can only call my parents on my free days to ask news about my children. The evenings are nightmares.

One evening after I finish taking care of the children, I race to get to my misery room, and twist my toe on stairs. The pain is unbearable. But I cannot scream, nor cry. I can only cry inside of me. I fear that if the children's mother hears that I have injured my toe, she will fire me. Losing this job would deepen the guilt of leaving my children far away.

After four weeks, though, I am dismissed from this family. No one tells me the reason why the mom decided to let me go. Maybe the telephone conversations with my Georgians friends and talking in a different language had something to do with it. Or maybe the broken coffeemaker was the reason.

Maybe I experienced too much culture shock. Maybe the family did.

∅

For three weeks I search for a new job. Every day seems like a century. I am not making money, and I feel guilty to disappoint my family.

Then I am hired to take care of an Italian couple. Old Ralf is eighty-six years old, but he doesn't look his age. When he was younger, he managed the bar business in City. Because of this, the house is full of bar decorations. The plates, cups, and a variety of souvenirs with his business logo. The basement's walls are covered with images of attractive women.

Ralf is kind, and his wife, Barbara seems to be an honorable woman. Her fine hands and red manicures give her very sophisticated look. She smiles at me.

Ralf tells me, "Barb has been sitting in this wheelchair, paralyzed, for seven years. She has changed many nurses during this time. The illness has not spoiled her character, though! She's a tough woman full of hope."

Soon I discover this for myself. Many times she encourages me with her words and actions. She becomes an example for me of a spiritually strong woman.

Ralf and Barbara's five children are very caring of their parents. Each one of them has chosen their day, and so every day someone comes to see their parents. They bring food, flowers, entertainment, and give much love to their mother.

Mostly my job is to look after Barbara. She needs help with many things—dressing, getting up, and lying down. It is not easy; I need a bit of strength to help her get up.

The family treats me with respect and kindness, but it is still hard for me to live with this routine. Accustomed to a free life, I feel locked up like a princess in a tall castle.

Ever since childhood I have loved to ask a million questions, and especially in this new country there are so many things I want to learn about. So I ask Ralf questions.

"Why are you asking so many questions?" he finally says. "No one before asked me so much. They simply came and took care Barbara."

But what can I do? How can I endure not to speak? I would go crazy! And so I continue to ask questions.

The couple's caring children treat me as their sister. Especially Patricia the oldest daughter, becomes very close to me.

One day Patricia hands me a novel. "Maka, you love reading, so I brought you something to read." Since then she has been supplying me with books.

"How are your boys doing?" she asks every time she comes to visit.

After I have been taking care of her parents for many weeks, she says, "I still can't understand how you could leave your boys with your parents and come to a strange country. How can you stand to be without them?"

I try to explain the political situation and unrest, the uncertainty of present and future self-reliance that leads us to search for better hope. But how can one truly understand what one has not experienced?

The most painful part of caring for Ralf and Barbara, though, is when Ralf's great-grandchildren come to visit. I play, laugh, and joke with them, but while I do my soul is crying for my babies who are somewhere far away in this huge world.

Days later, I decide I need to get outside whenever work allows. There is a school building on the corner of the street. I start running in the modern stadium for the compensation of missing my family and distracting myself. When Ralf gives me the sign of the light at the door, I return home. This district is close to the famous Chicago O'Hare International Airport, and the planes constantly fly over the stadium.

Once while jogging, I look up to the sky, to an airplane flying east, toward Europe. Unintentionally, my thoughts follow it and go all the way to my home, to my boys. Momentarily I feel some relief! I feel great! I continue my dream. I hug my little angels and my tired parents, caretakers of those restless boys. I feel at home. My burdened soul starts to breathe again.

Then I see a second plane in a different part of the sky. It is flying the opposite direction, from the east toward Chicago. My thoughts arrive on the American land again, bringing me back to reality.

As many more days go by, those imaginary visits save me from loneliness and nostalgic melancholy.

☙

Gradually I have come to know some local rules and traditions. I am still discovering others.

One day we go together to visit relatives. Everyone greets me warmly, but soon all of them become busy hugging, laughing, talking, and eating various kinds of Italian dishes.

Hmm, I am also hungry. I want someone to offer me food. On the assumption of Georgian hospitality, I wait for someone to come and invite me to the feast.

Several minutes pass. I guess no one is going to do it.

I notice that everyone feels free—if they are hungry, they take food, eat, and continue to entertain each other.

I am hungry too, but we are not used to directly expressing our feelings or wishes. Even if we are hungry, we refuse several times the proposed delicious dish, and then with great reverence we help ourselves.

I am left without food.

Back home again with Ralf and Barbara, I still try to understand my collision with reality. Finally, I realize that Americans are far from any false behavior. But since I hate everything that is for show, I don't think of this as a tragedy.

From now on, when I go somewhere, I will not expect someone to beg me to eat. I will help myself.

※

Many Americans do not have an understanding of what is behind the scenes of being an emigrant, being a nanny or caregiver, behind the money we earn and send home to countries to make our loved ones happy. Behind all of this is the pain of possibly becoming lost in the universe, and the constant fight not to let that happen.

I feel this burden strongly one day, as I overhear Ralf talking with the nurse who has come for a casual check on Barbara. He talks about me and all emigrants.

"They are lucky to come to this country. See, she lives here and doesn't have to do too much. They make easy money and support their families overseas. We give them so much of everything." Ralf goes on and on about how lucky I am.

A feeling like fire starts burning my whole inside.

After the nurse leaves, Ralf notices the change in me. He asks me to share.

"Ralf, you are thinking that we are the lucky ones to be here, work, make money, and support families. Yes, we are, *and* we are not. Imagine you can't see your children for six months. Imagine you miss your parents, friends, close ones. You are among strangers, in what is for you a strange culture. You have not been sentenced, but in a way it seems like you were sentenced. You have to do it in order for your loved ones to survive hardship. And yes, I am thankful to all of you, but I also need people like you to understand that this comes with a high cost for us. Each penny we secure with the blood in our veins."

He is left in astonishment after my revelation.

※

Even though Ralf is grumpy when I talk a lot and ask many questions, I know he cares about me as a person. This is a very good feeling. But my free-spirited personality still feels like the princess kept in a high castle, unable to go out freely. I also miss my children. Guilt feels like broken glass inside me for being away from them for so many months.

I make a decision. *I am returning to Georgia and will not look back to America!* According to the American rule of resignation, I inform Ralf about my leaving two weeks ahead.

Poor old man! For four months he repeated over and over that I was talking too much, but now he becomes upset and gets frightened.

During the next two weeks he knocks on my room door every morning. He says, "I will pay money for the phone, but call your mother and tell her you are staying for a while." He is worrying; he will have nobody to talk to about interesting topics. He has come to enjoy Georgian hospitality.

This commitment of Georgian women is common in this foreign country. Those we work for feel our maternal care, dedication to housework, and warm hearts. Therefore, the families we work for entrust their homes and children and parents to us.

Then we make friends with these families, and they allow us to bring guests and friends to their houses. We accordingly are more grateful, and with more desire we take good care of their children and parents. Then the elderly get used to us and find it hard to part from us.

I will miss this family also. But my own family has been far away for much too long.

I pack my belongings to return home to Georgia.

Chapter Nine
Losing Identity

Back in Tbilisi, Georgia
September 2000

After a six-month separation from my family, I return home to Georgia.

I tell my family, "I do not ever want to leave here again!" I make a firm decision. This is the end of searching. I will stay.

Six months spent alone in thoughts have brought another clarity in me: I do not want to waste any more time in worthless conflicts with my husband.

"We will not be together!" I tell David on the first day.

Obviously it is shocking for him. "Let us try," he asks. "Maybe we can improve our relationship!"

I think that at least David is trying to save the family, which hasn't been a family for a long time. After some discussion, I agreed to try, to start new steps slowly.

However, this is an irony of fate. The next morning, after he takes the kids to kindergarten, he does not return home.

An hour later he telephones. "Maka, pack my things. I have decided not to come back."

I am delighted to pack his things. Our struggle of living as a married couple has come to an end.

If America is a culture shock for some of the newly arrived Georgians, no less funny stories happen back here in Georgia, after we are accustomed to the rapid pace of the American way of life.

I am in Georgia. I need a job and stability to get used to this place again. But it is 2000, and not easy to find a job.

Here and there have appeared newly launched businesses and shops. I am told that a new supermarket has opened near my house. I think I will try out the fates.

I approach the polished shop and enter. My smiling face meets several serious, frowning girl's faces. I feel as if someone has grabbed my shoulders and shaken me.

I introduce to them the reason for my visit and inquire about the conditions.

One says that the working hours are from eight in the morning to eight at night. The salary is four GEL.

"The salary is four GEL per hour, is not it?" Innocently I seek to confirm.

"Do you think you are in America?" The girls look at me mockingly.

I leave the place without looking at them again. The job pays approximately $1.60 United States dollars for twelve hours of work. That is roughly 13 cents per hour in US currency.

Maybe I do think I am really in America? Again I feel my shoulders shaken. I've identified with American experiences for months. It will be very hard for me to get back to old thinking.

For days I try to get a job. People often say to me that slogan, "Do you think you are in America?" I see that slowly I am losing my place among my people—at home, in my country.

Eventually these words, "Do you think you are in America?" awakens the idea of going back to America.

I have gone. Then I have come back again. And gone. And come back. Each time I have gone, I knew I did not wanted to be without my children, and I come back again.

Losing my place in my country is hard. Trying to find it in a new land among strangers is even harder. While spending six months at a time in two contrasting cultures, my conscience is put on a scale.

Accustomed to American smiles and friendly relationships with people, you think it is the same in your own country. Back in Georgia, distrust, lies, unemployment, lack of money, harshness, and gloomy expressions hurt you like a slap in the face.

In Georgia, I am asked many times the question full of sarcasm: "Do you think you are in the United States?" Getting tired of all this, I feel an invisible rope pull me slowly back into that distant point of light, America.

∅

Chicago, Illinois
March 2001

Things in Georgia are not working out. I also feel out of place. One day I decide I will go back to America again.

"I thought you were not going back there anymore?" Katie, my friend, asks me with worry.

"Yes, I said that. But I don't see any point to working forty to fifty hours a week, not see my children, and after a month make only one hundred dollars. This is not enough to buy food for a week. I'll be back in six months." I say this with great confidence, but I am not sure that everything will work out. I still need to get a visa.

I continue on with my plan. My parents agree again to take care of the boys for another six months without me.

In the spring of 2001, I return to Chicago. One of my Georgian friends helps me to find place to live. Everything is familiar already, and I feel very confident.

I go back to Lena. The first day, she sends me on two job interviews. I am offered a job at both places at the same time. Then I know clearly: Earlier, families had to choose me. From now on, I will choose myself which position I like better.

My choices are babysitting for three children in a suburban house, live there, and have a quiet life . . . *or* taking care of a three-week-old infant in an affluent neighborhood of Chicago, going there each day from seven in the morning till three in the afternoon, and afterward breathing the city excitement!

I choose city excitement. Lake Michigan is just ten minutes away! Who cares about suffering during transport to my job? The main thing is that I will be here, where life is in full swing! The infant's mother is editor of a newly started magazine. What better job and family I could wish for?!

My neighborhood is populated with young professionals. Every morning I wake up at five o'clock. My route to work requires a ten-minute walk to the bus station, a bus ride to the train, and then transit on the train to my destination. I do not mind the ninety minutes of transportation. I have a book to read, and the time is used purposefully. The train gives me experience to get used to a diversity of people. Everyone looks busy going to work. Some carry hot coffee in hand—

This American style of carrying coffee everywhere is so strange, I think. Nobody in Georgia would leave home with hot or cold drinks, or with food. We are taught manners. Don't these people have manners?

Time goes by, and I find myself carrying coffee with me on the train ride. *Well, with this fast-paced life and long rides, you need to have a hot drink, I guess.* I find an excuse and an explanation.

Cultural differences fascinate me. I examine, compare, and judge, but all this is food for my curiosity.

On the train some people read books, like I do. Others work on their open laptops. Some talk on the phone, mostly about business. People are various kinds of race, looks, and clothing.

Finally, after an hour and a half trip, I step off the train into the golden June sun. I walk along the road, and in five minutes I am at work.

On Fullerton Avenue the price of land is very expensive. Therefore, the houses are built one after another. There is not enough parking area. I have fun watching from the window how drivers try to park between other compact cars.

You have to be very quick to park your car in the city, and when you do you are always afraid to get a fine! But this kind of thing often happens. I have more than once tasted the bitterness of paying the fine, and have paid fifty to seventy dollars with a trembling hand only, because I did not read the sign properly introducing the time, for example, of cleaning the street from fall leaves at a certain place. Then you park your car and get a fine.

The baby's mother, Susan, and I become close friends. On the warm summer days, we take the baby out for walks together. During our conversations I try to absorb like a cloud all information the editor tells me about internal matters of the magazine. It reminds me of my profession and first jobs after graduating from the university, when I used to work for newspapers.

"Our magazine mainly advertises new products on the market, in the areas of beauty, fashion, perfumery, and many others."

Advertising companies present their products to Susan, as an editor, hoping for good writing. There are new Fossil sports watches, Lancôme cosmetic bags, accessories of foreign design, newly made perfumes, teddy bears, picture frames, and other strange items. I am also given a lot of gifts from this broad choice of things.

This job is different from a live-in one. I have more freedom. In the emigrant terminology, it is called "come and go," which means to work in the daytime, but at night you can go home.

One day I have to find different place to live, so I contact my previous job, the elderly family from Italy. I had a close relationship with them and hope they might give me one room for rent.

"Maka, we need to think about insurance and all details. What if suddenly a fire starts?" Bob, Ralf's older son, is in charge of the house.

"Bob, I am such a careful and responsible person!" My answer is honest, and they know that too.

After a family discussion, they agree to let me live in one room.

Angela, my Moldovan friend, still works in their home. Months ago when I left the country, I suggested to Ralf to hire her, and he did. Now Angela and I will be roommates. All seems to be working out great.

I move in and adjust to my new room. I try to justify their confidence and not to damage anything.

Then there is one morning. Being far from family and homeland, I always have a candle and a painting of St. Mary and Jesus. I pray silently on my own, praying to God for my family's welfare. Unfortunately, I do not have a candlestick and use a small plastic holder instead.

Suddenly, the doorbell rings. I rush to the door, and let my friend in for coffee. Busy with conversation, all of a sudden we hear the voice of the installed emergency sirens.

"What's going on?" Confused, we run about but cannot find what is happening, why the device has been launched. The same device is installed in all houses and buildings, and even in case of a slight smoke, an alert informs residents about the threat.

I pray to God that the police do not come and the family does not know about this.

Suddenly I remember the candle! I rush into my room. The candle is melted, the plastic holder is as well, and the table surface has a small trace of burn.

It is a very small burn mark. I do not believe anyone ever notices it. I am even more careful after this.

✿

After one month I am done working at Lincoln Park. The free evenings have given me a taste of working in city and being able to visit places like the Lincoln Park Zoo and the Art Institute of Chicago. Now it is time to settle in one place and work toward the plan to go back to my boys in five months.

At this time Angela decides to visit her country. She asks, "Maka, would you like to take care of Barbara in my place for a few months, while I am visiting my parents?"

"This can work perfectly," I said. She would be gone almost five months. After her return, my six-month period would expire and I would go back home.

We agree.

Chapter Nine—Losing Identity

Days pass without excitement. Then I wake the morning of September 11, 2001.

The morning starts regularly. Before I go to wake up Barbara, I shower then have free time to enjoy coffee and a quiet morning. In the kitchen, while I fill the coffee pot with water, my eyes look through the window into infinity. My thoughts always go farther than just view in front of me. *I wonder what the boys are doing now. Are they sleeping? They must be bigger now. Will I recognize them?* I mechanically turn toward the coffeemaker, pour the water inside, and turn it on.

In a few moments, the fresh and inviting smell of coffee fills the room.

I continue to follow my routine. I push the TV on button and start to prepare medication for Barbara. The newsperson on TV is talking nonstop. Suddenly I look at screen. Smoke is curling up from a skyscraper.

Again, some stupid movie, I think, paying it little attention. I pour coffee into my cup and take a sip.

"Mmm." A feeling of pleasure goes through my body along with the coffee. I sit on a chair by the table, take a relaxed breath, and look at the screen again.

The smoke has intensified, and the movie scene hasn't changed.

Something is really going on.

Alarm seizes me. I turn the volume up and start listening anxiously. Fear grows inside me as I watch.

The ring tone of the phone makes me jump.

"Hello?"

"Maka, it's Natia!" My Georgian friend is calling from a neighboring state. "Are you watching TV? This is really happening. Terrorists are bombing New York."

I wake up to the full, horrible reality. Scared to death, I hang up from Natia, grab my calling card, and with shaking hands dial the long number. I am calling home.

"Mom, this is me."

"Maka? Are you okay?"

"Yes, yes. Terrible things are happening right now, but thank God we are okay in Chicagoland. Don't worry."

September 11 is a shock in Americans' peaceful lives. Before this, most of their interests have centered around their homes, families, and their cities or towns, not dangers such as this.

For me, it is the worst experience of my American journey. The beacon of hope to oppressed people around the world has been attacked, in an attempt to destroy that hope.

But in the weeks that follow, the people of the United States only become more caring of each other, and more patriotic to their nation.

※

Maybe it is ironic that in English vocabulary, a non-American is called an "alien," which has the second meaning as "a creature from outer space." I believe we are thought of so.

What is worse is I sometimes feel this way. Until 2003, I travel between Georgia and the United States, back and forth, back and forth. The United States remains an alien culture to me in many ways, as mine is to them. I miss my sons and return to Georgia, always certain I'll never leave my homeland again.

But every time I return in Georgia "for good," full of new ideas and desires, the close-minded remarks of my countrymen block my inspiration. For sure, it is the result of communist upbringing. Having grown up in framed thinking, I cannot find the courage to implement my own ideas or ignore the negative comments and hopelessness of others. Instead, I wait for approval from my fellow Georgians. It does not come.

I leave America in 2003 and return to Georgia with the decision of putting an end to my travel between the two continents (once again, how many times!!!). I feel I cannot continue like this. I will put an end to missing my children, to my children's going to school alone, to the missed period of their growth, naughtiness, joys, and thoughts. I will not be able to return those years, and I do not want to miss any other thing from their lives.

I am in Georgia for a year. Am I starting to think again about another trip to the United States?

My views and thoughts are still blocked by the reactions of hopeless people. I have never in my life given up, and now, after gaining so many experiences in America, it is difficult for me to follow the slow flow of life in Georgia.

I am losing identity. I now belong to neither country, yet to both. To neither culture, yet to pieces of each of them. I feel fulfilled within my family home. But I feel alone, like a foreigner, outside its walls.

I am losing myself.

Chapter Ten
In It Together

Tbilisi, Georgia
May 5, 2004

A year ago, when I was leaving the United States, I said to myself, *I am never coming back to America again!* I was tired of missing my sons, my parents, and my homeland. I told the people I worked for, Patrick and Helen, my decision.

Patrick said, "All right, Maka. Go back to your family, hug them, and take care of things. And when you decide to come back, bring your boys with you to this country. You are always welcome in our family. Your boys and Alex can play together, and everything will be great!"

"Thank you, Patrick," I said in heartfelt appreciation, "but I am never coming back here again."

Well, as the saying goes, "Never say never." Here I am, after spending a year with my three sons, telephoning Patrick and Helen with a question. The job at their house is still waiting for me.

∅

By eight in the morning, I arrive at the United States consulate, which by this time is so familiar to me. For my two younger sons and myself, I had applied for visas to America. Today would be my interview. Today I would learn whether we would be allowed to go to that country of hope together.

Finally, it is my turn! I let out a breath of release then enter the doorway.

I am directed to a small room. Inside, five guards stand by security cameras and check everyone who enters.

One of them politely addresses me. "Take out your passport and put your purse here, please."

I hand my passport to him, feeling very happy. I am confident I will be granted the three visas for my sons and myself.

A professional-looking young man flips through my passport and the application form. Then he frowns. "Whose pictures are these?" he asks. "Are these children trying to apply for visas too?"

"Yes." I felt something unpleasant sink inside of me.

"Where are they?"

"They are at home," I answer with fear.

"Well, everyone who is applying should be here! You need to bring them here."

After a crazed taxi ride during which I collect Nika and Sandro, we return to the consulate. We are given three visas.

When we arrive back home, I learn that Levaniko wants to come with us.

Two days later, I return to the consulate and am given a visa for Levaniko too.

Soon, all four of us bounce about in excited preparations for our upcoming travel. . . .

⌘

We change planes for our eleven-hour trip from Athens to Chicago and find our seats in a huge Boeing. There are quite a few small children on board.

A family, an American father and a Greek mother with three young children, sits right next to us. All six of our children play well together hour after hour, and for me it makes time go a little faster.

Four Georgians have left their homeland and are flying to a different continent. The goal is to come back to Georgia after six months. No one knows, though, where invisible ropes of destiny will take us. Deep down in my heart, I am distraught. I wish my country would not let me go from its caring hands to fight unknown, upcoming difficulties. Unfortunately, Georgia remains unable to take care of its citizens. Like my young sons and me, many others now face emigration struggles, fraught with nostalgia.

After eleven hours we land in New York City. "Children, say good-bye to your new friends!" All of us are packing our loose belongings and thanking each other as we prepare to leave the plane.

"Let's go, everyone," I tell my boys. "Be attentive, follow me, look after each other, make sure we all stay together." As I make all the short demands, I feel pretty strong and sure of myself. These steps are now easy to me, familiar. I do not fear any problem rising before us. We leave the airplane.

With strong steps I follow the people and signs, holding hands on my boys and constantly keeping an eye on them. It is always there, my attention. We reach the check-in counter.

The long line of people waiting for their passport checking is amazingly organized. The boys look entertained with so many different appearances of people, suitcases, colors. It is very interesting sightseeing.

"Hey, look, our friends!" Levan sees the familiar family parallel to us in the other line.

I look over at them, and we smile to each other. Deep inside of me, a small fear begins trembling. What if something goes wrong in America? But I push it back, trying to make it disappear.

Suddenly, the father of the children separates from his members and walks toward us. "Hi, boys. Here you are on American land! Welcome, and let this journey be happy for you. Have this small gift from us for a fun start. Good luck to you all." He hands a five-dollar bill to each of the boys, turns around, and then begins walking back to his family.

Our eyes follow him and see his three little children and their mom proudly and happily watching their dad walk to them. They all know what a kind act he just did. I overflow with happiness. As usual, my mind momentarily thinks for a next move.

I turn to my excited sons. "Hey, guys, you have some small toys in your collection. Why don't you choose three and quickly run and give them to your new friends, who just gave you such an unexpected gift."

The boys do not need another word. They search inside their backpacks. In a minute they are handing toys to their small acquaintances. The parents have a pleased smiled on their faces. Our eyes meet. This is a moment of gratitude without words.

A minute later we go through passport checking and cross the border.

I busily figure out which direction to go to find our last plane, to Chicago. Physically I make sure every second that the boys are with me, but I completely forgot about emotional side of this quite enormous travel. My emotions remind me now. The huge airport is filled with people everywhere.

"Let's go, boys, hurry up. We need to find our gate. Let's go!" I am sure to sound cheerful as I encourage them on and walk with a fast pace.

All of a sudden, Nika goes toward chairs and sits there.

"Nika, what are you doing, dear?" I mechanically ask, not having an idea what a hurricane is about to hit me.

"I am not going to America. Take me to my grandma. I don't want to go to America." Nika's stubborn voice is very definite. Tears run over his lower eyelids and flow down his cheeks.

"What?" Still not quite realizing what he is saying, my voice trembles. *What should I say? We are already in America. There is no way I can take him back to Grandma.*

I feel confused and lost. I realize I have to slow down.

"Nika, dear, everything will be good. I'll buy candies, we'll ride on rollercoasters, let's go now, let's walk." I try to bribe him, not quite telling him that this is already America. We still have one more flight to Chicago, and I cannot afford Nika's rebellion. As well, I am scared. What if Sandro and Levan start refusing?

A hug and love melt the little boy's loving heart. He wipes his tears and gets up.

I hold his hand silently, and we proceed ahead.

☼

"Boys, hold on, we need to check our tickets here." We reach the airline booth. I hand over my tickets and let out a deep breath. Just moments ago I had a huge obstacle rising with Nika's near rebellion, but, thank God, I managed. With this thought I calmly wait for the gate directions. But I guess it was already starting: waterfalls of obstacles for me to overcome.

"Miss, your flight is delayed," the calm and professional representative tells me. "You need to book the next flight, and be sure to get a hotel room as well."

"What do you mean? Why it is delayed? When will be our next flight?" I bomb her with questions.

"The next flight will be in the morning, ma'am." Her calm voice does not change. "There is huge storm in Chicago."

"But the airline should pay for our hotel! I am not going to pay." I try to win the argument. Spending three hundred dollars is not in my budget, and I try to save anyway I can from this unexpected expense.

"Miss, the airline does not pay for delays caused by natural events. You need to book your room as soon as possible, because in two minutes will pour an ocean of people also delayed, and then all hotels will be booked. You need to pick up your luggage first, in baggage claim, and then book the hotel." She really tries to help.

Suddenly I hear a noise, and look back. She is right! Hundreds of passengers are coming toward us with a racing speed. She gives us directions to baggage claim.

"Okay, boys, we can do this. You just need to be attentive, follow me, and be helpful. We are strong, right?" I realize I have no choice. We move away from the counter and head to baggage claim.

After we load up our cart, we push open the big glass doors to outside. The breath of New York City hits my nose. *I have to be strong.* We push the cart, all four of us. The boys are understanding, knowing they cannot complain. This is no time for Nika to be childish, even though he is eight. We have to be resilient in this strange place.

We push. Suddenly raindrops start falling on our heads, wetting us. It seems the sky is crying instead of me. We push, then there is a small rise, so we have to push harder. "Okay, boys, a little more, it's all good. . . ." I keep speaking words of encouragement as I push against the cart, as I push against the difficulties of life.

"Are you Georgians?"

I hear someone asking in our native language. I turn around. A young man and woman stand in front of us.

Suddenly all my strength collapses. I shed tears. My tears join the rain. Now we are both crying: the sky and me.

"Why are you crying?" The confused couple try to understand my frustration. "We watched you arguing with the airline representative—you seemed so tough. You and your boys are in safe hands now. We are here to help you. You can stay with us tonight, then we will put you into a cab, and you can catch the flight in the morning."

Is that God watching over us? Is that God giving his helping hand to us?

Definitely!

For the remainder of the day, the caring character of the Georgian people manifests itself. At the couple's small apartment, they feed us and give us a place to sleep. They call the cab for us at four the next morning and pay the taxi driver for our ride to the airport as well.

"Hey, boys, have these small trucks. You can play with them when you are traveling." They hand them small toy trucks.

Boys are boys. They become interested in the details of the toys and playing. Further travel is less stressful. I am thankful for the caring side of Georgian's nature.

∅

Chicago, Illinois

When we land in Chicagoland, we know Uncle Levan will be waiting in the airport to meet us, and will be happy to get to know the twins he never met before.

Nika completely forgot about his breakdown yesterday, and bounces more than walks off of the plane, anxiously waiting to see his never-seen uncle. Sandro and Levan too are excited. After all the procedures of security checking and baggage claim, glass doors automatically part in front of us, opening the road of possibilities and opportunities.

"Uncle Levan, Uncle Levan!" The boys recognize him right away. They already know him from pictures. Little Levan acts mature and confident. He personally met his uncle few years ago, and that gives him more self-assurance.

After all our greetings, Uncle Levan guides us to the parking garage.

"This is my car." Uncle Levan points at his old green Mercury Tracer wagon.

I recognize my old car, which I bought for one thousand dollars on a previous trip to America. It is now Levan's.

The boys check out the car. In Georgia our family never had a car, so this is a very exciting moment for the boys. This is the first "their" car. They see all the outside of the car, then we climb into it.

In my seat I sit back, and Uncle Levan drives. The boys ask all kind of questions to their uncle about the car, streets, buildings, America, toys . . . just anything.

Finally, I can relax from being responsible. I unconsciously turn that position over to my brother, close my heavy eyelids, and doze.

Uncle Levan got divorced from Janet and moved from Minneapolis to this Chicago suburb one year ago. Now his new apartment is located in a nice neighborhood, not far from Chicago O'Hare Airport. Our plan is to stay with him.

"McDonald's!" someone yells from the backseat. This is a familiar sign which connects them to their own city, their own loved places. Their happiness makes me happy too. I know if there are sad moments of nostalgia of missing Georgia, these places will help us out.

The family I worked for one year on my previous visit await me to take me back to work, the family with four children in an upscale neighborhood. Luckily I find out about a summer school ten minutes away from Levan's place, and a week after our arrival in America, my boys join the park district summer school, from nine in the morning to three o'clock, at an unbelievably affordable price. On Monday morning Sandro, Nika, and Levan are ready for the new experiences.

"Guys, don't run on the stairs! You are making too much noise!" But my voice is lost among feet pounding as three energetic and excited boys run downstairs.

Levan's car enters the gated entrance of the neighborhood. The beautifully and neatly mowed green grass, trees, and perfect houses are nothing like the boys have known from their childhood memories in Georgia.

"Welcome to our camp!" A pretty young camp advisor greets the boys with a kind and warm smile on her face.

The boys have no hesitation in staying in this completely strange environment. The boys speak only the Georgian language, except Levan who knows a few core words in English. It is brave of them to enter into the different culture, strange people, unfamiliar settings, and not knowing the language to talk and play. It is brave of me to leave them here and to hope they will adjust without any problem. But the interesting thing is that children tend to adjust quickly and easily, using instincts and body language to understand each other.

Right away the boys start to interact with American children and the English language.

All is going great. Within a few weeks of arriving, I have a job, the boys are busy in the summer camp, and we have a nice place to live. But as soon I am ready to take a deep breath of relief, at least for some time, I hear the phone ring.

"Hello, Maka," the landlord says. "I'm sorry to tell unpleasant news to you. Neighbors are complaining about too much noise the boys are making. You can't stay at this place. I can offer you an apartment in the basement because you've been a very good tenant."

Any attempt to keep quiet three energetic boys, who have just arrived from a country where they had enormous freedom to play outside, has been ineffective. The walls of our condo in Tbilisi, like all condominium apartments and houses in Georgia, are thick. They are built out of bricks and blocks and therefore are more soundproof. We lived on the first floor and had no one living underneath us. Well, here in Chicago everything is much different. The apartment with wooden walls and floors do not keep out the sound. Neighbors get disturbed from the noise of running and jumping boys.

The thunder roars in a clear sky.

"What? We can't stay?" Moving out means paying rent, and how am I going to do this all by myself?! I am ready to collapse.

But with the same speed of thunder, a calculator in my head starts computing my life. Such is the conclusion: Even though my brother is supporting me, moving closer to my job would be the best outcome from the existing situation.

When my brother returns home and I tell him, he promises to be there for us.

I start the search for a new place to live. The first house I read about is the one! It sounds perfect for our conditions. It is a single house, divided into four small apartments, in a nice neighborhood, and is closer to work. The boys will have the yard to run around and can even walk to school.

My hand is still shaking in excitement as I sign the lease. We move to Des Plaines, Illinois.

Then, using my past experience of how to furnish the place with secondhand furniture, we start checking garage sales. The boys have bliss as they find all kinds of toys and small things among old treasures to entertain themselves. I am happy too that I can keep them occupied at an affordable price.

Soon our one-bedroom apartment is furnished with secondhand furniture from garage sales, friends, and from people who put out unneeded furniture pieces on the curb. And most importantly, we have a vehicle. The green Mercury Tracer comes back into my ownership.

We have mostly everything to satisfy our essential needs except a bed. One day at a garage sale, I find it.

"What? Is this a water bed?! I have never heard of it. Well, we need one, so we should get it."

A water bed turns out to be an extraordinary thing, and it's big enough to fit all three boys. They have fun every night on the mattress filled with water that moves like waves. It adds excitement to their lives, and their happy laughter fills our new home.

Sometimes so little is needed for real happiness! Funny moments like these balance the stressful days.

I work hard. Including my own, I have three families' problems to worry about. In the daytime I care for an eighty-two-year-old lady, Mary. During evening hours, I help Patrick and Helen's household of four children. Between these two jobs, I cook dinner for my boys; by five in the evening, all four of us get into the car and drive to work, where my boys are welcome to play, study, and watch TV. They are able to stay with me every evening while I am busy taking care of the other family's children.

✵

Is it natural talent, or is it foreign language learning methods in natural settings, that by September, when my boys prepare to enter the elementary school, they can speak, write, and study in English?

Days pass by. I work, and the boys go to school. Everyone in our lives is very caring, helpful, and friendly.

The elementary school where the boys go is in walking distance in a quiet neighborhood. There are a few small streets to cross, and the school crossing guards help children to cross them. This is something we aren't familiar with, as there are no special people in Georgian streets to help children to cross the busy city streets so they can safely reach the school.

I feel very safe to send the boys to school by themselves. Every guard is nice, but one of them becomes special.

One day I accompany the boys to school. A lady guard greets us warmly, and the boys smile back at her. Suddenly she hands me a small piece of paper with her address on it.

"Boys, here is my address. Can you please stop at my house after school? I have bicycles for you. My three boys have grown up. They don't need those bikes, and you can use them. Please come and pick them up."

I look at the boys and see three pair of eyes sparkling with happiness and joy. Huge smiles shine in their faces. I feel they can hardly stay still. They want to get those bikes right away. Back at home they didn't own bikes. Yes, they always shared friends' bikes, but between requests like, "Now it's my turn," "Just one more circle, please!" And now each of them will have his very own! And they will be able to ride bikes to school instead of walking!

After school we pick them up, big bicycles with nice wheels! Oh! What a wonderful day it is for them!

The bicycles make going to school every morning much easier and fun.

No doubt, experiences like this have a huge impact on children's inner worlds, and strengthens their values, because they learn from the generosity of kind families how to be generous.

In this way American culture is like Georgian. People give to each other and help one another. Maybe it is a trait of humanity to help our fellow man during life. To be in it together.

Chapter Eleven
"What Is Possible?"

After two years of living in Des Plaines, I feel it is time for some change. I like the area and the friends we have, but I want a bigger place and to give my boys new opportunities. It is not an easy decision to make, as I have to balance my expenses.

With great calculation and planning, I come to the conclusion that it is wise to move. I start the search and find exactly what I hoped for.

In this I see how God is always watching after us, always bringing the right thing when it is the right time.

For two weeks, on our way to my work, we fill my car, which is not the Mercury Tracer anymore, then drop everything in the new home, and continue to my work.

After we move in, the boys love the new place. I made sure to have a view from our balcony. The view is always more important for me than the place itself, because there is much more in life than our small inner world. From the balcony we see a swimming pool and a green yard. This is the life!

∅

I always keep records of my outgoings. That helps me to manage and have important things for my boys at the same time.

But we run into challenges there too. Three growing boys and their appetites are a task.

It is fall of 2006. The school year has just started. My teenage boys look a few years older than their ages. Tired of making lunches for the past two years, I decide to let them eat at the school cafeteria. To make it even easier for myself, I activate an automatic payment from my bank account. But the bank account statement one month later is pretty shocking for me.

"What? The school charged me $435 in the month of September? This can't be true." Frustrated, I right away dial the school office number.

"Hello?" I hear a nice voice.

"Something is wrong. I've been charged $435 for my boys' lunches. Can you please check?"

The nice voice puts me on hold. She checks the account and then comes back with an answer. "Everything is right. Your boys have eaten that entire amount."

I froze, suddenly realizing their appetite. "Thank you," I say quietly.

As soon as I hang up, I check their web account. And there is the list: sandwiches, snacks, milk, ice creams. . . . The list goes on and on.

That evening we have a family meeting. "Boys, I understand that you need to eat, but if you continue eating with the current speed, soon I will file for bankruptcy."

I go back to my old routine—making sandwiches at home.

☙

Life continues on. I stay busy working as a nanny, caregiver, and housekeeper; my boys are fed and taken care of; we have a nice place to live. For almost ten years my main concern has been the physical survival of my family, and searching for my inner self as well. For that purpose, I crossed too many miles between countries. I wasted lots of tears. And even now, I hurt to realize I've had no chance to use my true strengths and my full potential.

My regret and cries about this misfortune of fate have gone viral among my friends. In a corner of Patrick and Helen's kitchen is a tall wooden stool. Tired from my morning job, feeding my boys, and racing to Patrick's house to work through the evening, I often collapse on this wooden stool and weep in the Russian language with Angela, my Moldavian friend, who also works at the same hours. I sob bitterly, "*Poterialas Ia, poterialas.*" "I am lost, I am lost." I cry out loud about my uncertain future and unused potential of personal capacity.

There has to be more to my life than this.

༄

Something else is still missing in my life. And that is love.

The role of the family is strongly rooted in Georgian mentality. Divorce was not encouraged in my parent's generation at all, and even though some women are not truly happy who have irresponsible or hurtful husbands, they still keep the marriages for the children's sake. A woman who does divorce is judged from society as if it is her fault to have her family dissolve.

But not only that, the society is very severe toward her singlehood, and it ascribes her with many unpleasant adjectives, as if she is vulnerable for wrong relationships. Over the course of my life these views have gotten softer, but even I experienced judgment and unsupportive remarks when my decision about divorce was revealed. I was raised in a very loving family environment—my parents just celebrated their forty-sixth wedding anniversary—so being single has been a sad feeling. I have always longed for having someone with whom I could share interests, time, and make unforgettable memories together, to hold hands, and walk together on endless walks.

One day someone mentions Internet dating. *Hm, let me see what that Internet dating is?!* I say to myself and open an online account.

I find it is a somewhat intriguing and unfamiliar world of singles. After two days of checking the account and chatting with a few guys online, I figure out everyone knows what they are looking for on this site.

I do the same, with the outlook that only a relationship potentially leaning toward marriage seems acceptable for me.

Then I meet a man, about fifty-five years old. *Perfect!* I think, realizing the heaviness of my baggage and the life-experience stability that is possible with his age. All the best descriptions characterize him—a professor, smart, successful, good looking.... We make a date.

We have a nice conversation, at a nice dinner, in a nice restaurant. Driving back home, I feel weird, as if I'm shopping for a husband. *No, no, no. I cannot just pick some man to marry as if choosing a condiment at a grocery store.*

I study many men's profiles online. My excitement about finding the perfect man turns into a dark, confused uncertainty.

This is a wakeup call into my conscious: I realize that I feel sorry for myself for being a single mom.

I lower the age limit. Only ten years older could be my mate.

Before I meet with a prospective guy, we have conversations so that I have an idea about him, his interests, and what he is looking for in relationships. Based on how well it goes, I might agree to meet with him at a Starbucks or in other coffee shops.

Weeks pass by, dialogues take place, and dates happen, but the knight on a white horse still does not appear to save me from my singlehood.

One day after my morning work, I race to my second lunch date with a certain man. I enter the restaurant and find him sitting in a booth. I am a little upset because of one of my acquaintance's remarks.

My date notices my concern and kindly asks the reason.

"I am upset about how people can be discouraging and judgmental. I work hard, and yes, I have everything taken care of well: my boys, jobs, school, everything. And instead of encouraging and supporting me with their positive, cheering words, it seems that a few people are jealous. Even worse, sometimes they tell me gloomy comments. This bothers me."

"Hmm. . . . Have you looked into the mirror?"

"What do you mean?" I get a little concerned. *Do I have something on my face?* I look at him with confused eyes.

"Have you looked into the mirror lately? Listen to what you've just told me. You said that even though you are single, you work hard, you have everything and everyone around you taken care so well, that some people are jealous. Well, maybe you are someone to be jealous of? They wish they were able to do things as well as you do, but they can't. All they can do is to envy you. That's why they tell you negative remarks."

Instantly I feel the inside of me light up. Then in a second I feel like my awareness on things has rotated 360 degrees and I have awakened with a whole new outlook.

I now understand that those people's negative emotions are their weaknesses. They wish to be strong enough to make brave decisions and steps in life, but they haven't yet. And for their flaws I have blamed myself, but no longer. Suddenly I feel strength inside of me.

From this day on, everything changes in my life. I don't take anything personally anymore. I don't pay attention to people's negativity, even though it can unfortunately interfere in our lives. I have changed my reaction, and that has changed my life. I no longer feel sorry for myself.

One day I read the book of Don Miguel Ruiz, *The Four Agreements*. The second agreement of Don Miguel Ruiz says, "Don't take anything personally. Nothing others do is because of you. What others say and do is a projection of their own reality, their own dream. When you are immune to the opinions and actions of others, you won't be the victim of needless suffering."

After finishing the book, I feel even more relieved. It is the confirmation of my strength once and for all.

I am thankful to the man I met for the second date, for opening my eyes at a time I could not see the light.

※

Eventually I decide that I am just wasting time on online dating. So one day very firmly I tell myself, "You know what? I am okay with being single," and I log out of the account, happy to be done with it.

A few months fly by. I am busy with my life and do not think about online dating. Then one day, I get curious and check the account again. Maybe it was meant to be!

There is a note. "Maka, what a beautiful name! Where are you from?" Tom, a good-looking man ten years older than me, is writing to me.

I type back, "I am from Georgia! Just to let you know, I don't have the time for dating. I am very busy and my life is not fun. Maka."

It seems Tom has decided to show me some fun in life. In his second note, he talks about the raising rules and habits of his own three children. He also touches on the painful subject about my country, and that leads us to long conversations, history analyses, followed by talk about our children.

We decide to get together for a coffee date.

We meet in an upscale mall at Starbucks' the morning before Christmas. The holiday spirit is in the air, making everyone happy. I see the famous Starbucks' logo and walk in that direction. Tom is there waiting for me. He is in shape and looks younger than his age.

"Merry Christmas! We picked the best day for the date."

He orders two lattes, and we sit at a small table. All around us excited people are resting from their long shopping day of racing to buy last-minute presents for their loved ones.

Tom says, "I've brought two small presents for you, Maka." He hands me two nicely wrapped boxes. "You can open one now, please, and as for the second one, open it tomorrow by your Christmas tree."

I unwrap the flat box. A soft, burgundy-colored cashmere scarf slips from it.

The second, I discover Christmas morning, is a lovely pair of gloves. After Christmas we begin to date. For months our relationship goes forward and we get closer. In September we start to talk about becoming a family, though we are not yet engaged.

℘

The role and importance of my native Georgian language has remained an obstacle in my relationship with Tom, and the subject of an argument.

"Maka, if we continue our relationship, I ask that you speak English, not Georgian, when we are all together and your English will also improve" Tom says.

I think, *We are already pretty fluent in English. I don't know why he is worrying?!*

"When my grandpa arrived in America from Luxemburg, he told all his children, 'We should forget the German language and speak only English in this country,' " he adds to support his viewpoint.

"Tom, the Georgian language is very important for us Georgians. If forgetting it is the condition for our relationship, then you should know it right now that's never going to happen, even if that costs me our relationship!" Now, more than ever, I have to hold onto my roots and save my sons' and my identities.

The argument ends, but soon I face a harsh reality. Tom cannot get used to the fact that I talk with the boys in Georgian.

Thankfully, Tom quickly realizes that denying my ancestors' and family's language will not be the case, and gave up. Soon he decides to suggest to me another idea: to marry him.

On Christmas Eve of 2007, one year after our first date, my boys, my brother, and I are all invited to Tom's house. Tom's three children and my boys have a fun time together.

From our previous talks, Tom knows of Georgian traditions about engagements and asking the bride's father for her hand. When we are all near the Christmas tree, Tom says, "Levan and Levan,"—Tom addresses my brother and my oldest son—"I know that in Georgia when a man wants to propose to a woman, he is to ask her dad for permission. Well, Maka's dad is not here in America, so I would like to ask both of you for permission. I would like to marry her."

It is a very emotional moment. It makes me very proud, appreciated, and respected. My sons grow stronger and become men in a second.

I have thought of marriage as one little step from singlehood. But then Tom puts the engagement ring on my finger. Soon after, I realize that this will not be an easy step in my life.

※

One morning I lay motionless on my family room couch, staring at the ceiling with my eyes frozen onto one spot. Tom sees and realizes there is something going on in my mind.

"What's wrong, Maka?" he asks.

"Can we move to one house south from here?" I ask with a monotonic voice.

This thought is generated from the fear that the small town where Tom's house is located will be too far from this area where I am used to living, and where most of my Georgian friends live.

He didn't expect a question like this. The next morning he is still unable to say a word.

Now we are both aware that this will not be an easy journey: two different cultures, upbringings, values, and outlooks on things.

Even so, we get married.

※

The summer of 2008 is a hard alteration period for all eight members of my new family. When my boys—ages fourteen, twelve, and twelve—and I move into Tom's big house on June 1, Tom is away on an international business trip. Tom's daughters, Jaime, twenty-two, and Shannon, eighteen, and his son, Andrew, eleven, are at home.

A big, colorful sign greets us, nicely decorated with Shannon's creativity.

WELCOME MAKA, LEVAN, SANDRO, AND NIKA

Now I can settle down! My subconscious mind tries to calm me. The boys and I move in, and we all become one big family.

"Hey, guys, let's do some revising in this kitchen, before we add many things we brought with us," I declare, and we all agree.

For the last five years, Tom has been a single dad of three, so from my point of view the kitchen can definitely use a woman's touch.

I take charge. We throw away a lot of old, broken glasses and plates and many other useless things. I clean the cabinets. Soon the kitchen has a whole new look. Even though being a housewife is not my personality's characteristic feature, the natural instincts of a woman and mom take their toll. I assumed that I would be in charge of the kitchen. To my huge surprise, I discover that Tom wants to compete for the Chef title. From that moment, the struggles begin.

※

"Where are my boys? I am losing them!" I feel seriously scared in the large house. I am used to close interactions among my children, myself, and their grandparents, as all of us lived in Tbilisi in a two-bedroom condominium. The boys and I always shared a small room. My parents filled our household with wisdom, stories, and fables every day while the children played nearby and joked together. I could always see where they were and that they were safe. Now my sons have their own bedrooms and a whole large house where I can't always find them.

I am drowning in the haste of my new lifestyle. The good part is that combining two different cultures is bringing diversity under the same roof, broadening the views and outlooks of each member. But at the same time, it is not an easy adjustment for any of us. As a mother and wife again, my responsibilities have doubled.

Every morning my husband, Tom, races to get ready for work in a record short time, something that seems common in American culture. I am scared that the wind of his energy will blow me away, so I hide under the blanket until the tornado passes.

I feel lost in the difficulties of my married life.

At the end of summer, Tom offers me to attend with him a seminar that will be presented by global consulting company Gap International in Philadelphia, Pennsylvania. This company is doing consulting work with the management at Kraft International, where Tom works. Kraft International offers seminars to the families and friends of executives. Tom thinks the trip and seminar might help me to overcome the challenges of huge changes.

I agree, and in two weeks I'm dressed in business casual, on my way to Philadelphia.

On the first day, I find myself among very successful, confident people. Some of them own businesses, and some are executives—a woman who is director of New York jail, a man who leads a five-million-dollar company, and many more.

The seminar instructors explain to us very smoothly that our thoughts can change our lives. I hear their words, but they don't mean much to me right away.

Soon the instructors ask everyone to speak about the huge obstacles we are facing in our lives, businesses, and work.

"What is the big concern, the main problem you are facing at this point in your life?"

The lady director of the jail has to find ways to handle relationships with thousands of prisoners and her coworkers.

Someone else has to fundraise $50,000 for his company.

Another person has huge debt and is trying to figure out ways to solve that problem while keeping their important job and taking care of their family.

Someone needs more confidence to develop her marketing skills to grow her company's success.

And then comes my turn to stand up and speak up about my unbearable obstacle.

"My name is Maka. I have been a single mom with three boys, and we emigrated from Georgia. Three months ago I remarried, to an executive. My problem is that I have a big house where I feel I am losing my sons, my Georgian friends live one hour away, and my husband and I argue about being a boss in the kitchen."

Suddenly everything shakes. I feel so small. *What silly problems I am talking about! These people here have serious things to take care of, and who am I to complain about such small and meaningless concerns?*

This speech makes me realize I am making my life miserable with the way I am thinking, with the way I am looking at things. Well, things I've done and obstacles I've overcome in life are the proof that I am strong and do not give up.

On the second day, we have to come up with a motto that will give us strength and power from within. "I am a leader!" I write, because I know I am not going to let anyone tell me what to do.

"Okay, Maka. That is very good, but Tom is a leader too. Would you like to take control and be in charge of the whole family?"

"No, no, I would not like that. I like him to be a leader too."

"In this case, how about a motto like, 'Leaders leading together'?"

This is it! I know in a second that this is what I want in life and in my family—leaders leading together.

On the third day, I leave the seminar strong and confident, knowing how to make a clear plan and set steps to reach that goal.

Gap's talented instructors have broken down reality and shown how each of us create our own reality. Our reality depends on how we look at things, think of possibilities, and how we plan. The instructors have made everything so much clearer for me. They have made me realize how I have not been focusing in the right direction, which has prevented me from enjoying my life. And they have made me see that I can realize my full potential through new thinking, goals, and new actions.

Now I also understand that in my life I have made a lot of radical decisions, driven by the desire to create a new future, to improve my situation. And I haven't seen before how radical some of those decisions have been.

The seminar is a great eye-opening experience for me. I have been given a chance in life to gain experiences, learn new things, expand my horizons with new possibilities, and explore the power of positive thinking. Gap has added the dimension of asking, "What is possible?"

Chapter Twelve
Let Your Life Speak

Tbilisi, Georgia
Present Day

I push my chair back from the dining table, knowing I must leave. "Hey, girls, I am very tired. I also have to travel tonight. Please continue without me."

They beg me to stay, but I don't change my answer. I say good-bye and leave the restaurant where I met my longtime unseen friends. My parents are waiting for me at home.

Two weeks of visiting time in my homeland is always full of feelings of guilt, as I never spend enough time with my parents. It's hard to deny so many invitations and requests from my loved ones. Everyone wants to see me, even for a few minutes—to talk, to share, to laugh, to remember precious moments spent together, to plan next gatherings, and most of all to get inspired and encouraged by me and the things I have discovered in my new country.

In return they all fill me with love of the type it's impossible to get anywhere else, from anyone else. Leaving always brings a waterfall of emotions.

It's 12:00 a.m., and the streets of Tbilisi are mysteriously calm and peaceful. The city does not sleep, and no one else with it. I can hear joyful sounds from richly and creatively decorated restaurants. Here and there I see couples holding each other's hands, walking. Some people stand in a group outside a small store and smoke cigarettes. That they do with a great passion here.

I walk fast toward lined-up taxis, fast like in the American culture, I realize. Passengers are rare this late at night, so drivers relieve their boredom by getting out of their vehicles and gathering nearby, where they talk and smoke. *Seems like everyone smokes in this town, except me*, I think.

At the closest taxi, I open the door and sit down.

The driver quickly separates from his colleagues. "Good evening. Where are we going?" he asks me with an enthusiastic voice.

"Vake," I say, my own voice sounding indifferent.

"Five Lari." He professionally names the cost of the trip.

"Uhhh, five Lari! Four would not work? Five is too much!" I try to negotiate the price.

"What do you mean too much, Ma'am?! It's quite right, and also it's late at night too."

He is charging too much! But, is it worth it to argue for one Lari? He probably spends all day in the car to make a living for his family. . . . My thoughts compete with each other. A small battle boils inside of me.

Again I stand on the line of two countries crossing. One pulls me by my roots with its love and care, which I want to give back to, while another pulls me in its direction with a shining, better life for my children and better opportunities, which I must be able to afford.

Again I worry about being apart from my parents and my childhood friends, and most confusing is that I am still trying to find myself while I am torn between the two continents.

Then I make a quick decision. I have a plane to catch after I see my dad and mom.

"All right, here is five Lari. Please take me home." I shut the car door like shutting the door to doubtful thoughts and confusion.

The car drives smoothly through the lighted Tbilisi streets. I find myself cozy and disappear into the blurry lights.

"You don't own a car, do you?" Suddenly the driver breaks the silence. "You don't know the expenses of a car."

"I have and don't have a car, at the same time."

"Do you work here?" The driver is trying to figure me out. Apparently I seem somewhat odd to him.

"Here and there . . . both places." The question sounded strange, and so does the answer.

"Are you a guest here?" The driver can't satisfy his curiosity.

"I am a guest and a host, at the same time."

"You speak very strangely." The disappointed driver finally gives up.

"This life is very strange itself," – I conclude.

The car drives. I become lost in the shining lights again.

One more time I am getting ready to fly back to America. One more time I am leaving my homeland. Each visit to my country, followed by the logical act of going back to the country where I live with my husband and three adult boys, brings enormous pain.

It is the endless pain of homeland-less-ness, friends-less-ness, parents-less-ness that I experience in the United States. The people I leave behind are my air to breathe when I am floating in space, and my water when I become thirsty like in desert.

Yet in America I live each day with wings grown from the inner happiness of knowing that I am going to come alive.

I live with this pain inside, even after years of living in my new country. A longing for my homeland always resurfaces, reminding me of it.

I thought that frequent visits to my homeland would help, but on the contrary, they work the opposite. The wound is always open, always fresh, and always ongoing. It has no time to heal, as I am soon taking another trip to the place where my roots are connected deeply.

Tonight once again, I will go to Tbilisi International Airport and leave part of my soul behind.

✺

I push wide open the taxi door—"Thank you! Have a good night!"—then with quick steps I reach the entrance of my condominium building and push the iron door. I run the stairs to the third floor. There is no elevator in my building, but maybe that's what keeps people in shape here.

I ring the doorbell. The sweet musical ringtone instantly touches chords of feelings inside me. They don't take the shape of any particular memory, only thoughts of a peaceful and safe childhood. I loved listening to this ringtone every time I would come home from school. I would ring this bell and call, *"Mom it's me!"*

"Mom it's me! Open the door!" I call just the same way again.

My elderly mom's slow steps approach the door, and she opens it wide.

"I am home!" I announce cheerfully and hug her. *She is so short!* The quick, sudden thought goes through my mind, and I realize that as years have gone by I've had to bend over, more and more, to reach my mom's soft and warm cheek for a kiss.

"Come on in." Her voice, calm as ever, reassures me that this is where unconditional support awaits me, no matter how much time may pass.

She wears a soft, puffy green robe, which I brought for her as a present on one of my previous visits. She looks as cozy as everything else in this house . . . or maybe this is connected to that home feeling, where everything feels the most peaceful when you are closest to your roots.

"Mom, we don't have too much time before my departure. Let's go and have a tea. Where is Dad?"

Even though I ask this question, I know my dad will be sitting in his cozy armchair, by the small desk full of papers and books, and will be writing.

I look in the family room, and there he is as I pictured him. Rezo, now eighty-four—still full of young spirit, bright mind, and sharp with any topic—is lost in his writings. I recall how my brother, Levan, and I would type and proofread his handwritten papers for the publishers while we were growing up.

"Dad." I bend down and kiss him. As always, he is wearing his inseparable black French beret, which has already counted more than thirty years, along with his glasses, his signature style. His small mustache still sits under his nose.

"Come on, let's have a tea," I announce and go to the kitchen.

The rectangle-shaped kitchen, which is about twelve feet by four feet, with a six-foot-high ceiling—a pretty good size—strangely feels small to me. In fact, everything in this house seems smaller, compared with how I remember it all seemed fifteen or twenty years ago.

The wallpaper has gotten older too. Oh, I remember how Dad and I worked hard to glue that wallpaper to the wall, when the Soviet Union collapsed and we had to find ways to survive. Now it's faded like the memories over so many years, but still it's precious, because it is part of my growing stronger by overcoming obstacles.

Everything here has some magical touch, which awakens even more memories. The old gas stove has stood in that same corner since my childhood, when I was too small to reach the back burners.

The red kettle with white polka dots also flashes an old scene. My beautiful Aunt Thea gave it to my mom for a birthday present, as part of a twelve-piece kitchenware set.

"Maka, Levan, let's go to a movie." For Aunt Thea, a joyful and kindhearted woman who never married, my brother and I were like her own children. Her hazel-colored eyes and eagle-wing-shaped eyebrows expressed her beautiful soul and passion for life. Although as a child I didn't understand well, now I realize fully that she was one of so many women who sadly became victims of soviet closed-minded thinking: Women's role and only purpose, according to society's prejudice, was marriage, but love and feelings were not only discouraged, they weren't even subject to be mentioned. Aunt Thea was different. I think she just never met her knight and chose to stay single. Sadly, she left us suddenly at the age fifty-one.

I light the stove and put on the polka-dot kettle. It still looks new because Mom kept the whole set wrapped for many years. It has always been hard for me to understand why people keep things in cabinets. Every family has a cupboard for showcasing: The Germans and French display porcelain tea or coffee sets, and crystal wine or champagne glasses. Mostly these dishes are never used, just looked at. Is that soviet damage too? Maybe, because they were so hard to buy and no one wanted to use them so that they would not be broken. It is sad! Truly, the people who buy and love them rarely get to feel the joy of having tea of coffee from a precious china cup, unless special guests come to visit.

I look inside the cupboard. The beautiful tea set rests there, pink and light green flowers painted on softly graven porcelain. Drinking tea from these sophisticated cups puts you into a different mode. Maybe your sitting manners by the table would even be determined by their beauty and tenderness.

At the stove I pour hot water into the white porcelain teapot and call my parents. "Tea is ready."

"We are coming," Mom's soft voice replies from the family room, and I hear her good-naturedly trying to drag my dad from his papers.

"Just a moment, just a moment." Dad's cheerful voice is trying to steal one more second to write one more word or one more sentence.

Mom is first to enter to kitchen, as usual, since her curiosity is eager to hear something new from me.

Green tea aroma spreads throughout the room, inviting us into a peaceful, intimate evening. Then I breathe in the aroma through my nostrils. The scent warms up my whole body, giving me a pleasurable shiver that transports me into a past filled with similar memories. I long so much for this in my foster country, missing my home and memorable places.

Dad joyfully enters the kitchen. "Hmm . . . yummy!" he exclaims cheerfully.

I am sure heavy sorrow lies on both their hearts, as their children and grandchildren live thousands of miles, and vast oceans, away. But no! They will not show their sadness to me, and that makes my guilty feelings even bigger. Parents! How much they do for their children unconditionally. The more we grow, the more we understand.

My dad, mom, and I talk for a while.

"I am working on my next book," Dad says and tells me details about his plans.

I recall the book he worked on for so many years, but which he could never publish, or even dare to mention, until the Soviet Union fell. *The Story of the Repressed Family* sits on his bookshelf now, and on many bookshelves in the region. The title still makes me shiver. The horrible history of communism and their cruel footsteps in Georgia runs one more time in my mind, making me appreciative I've been born, and that my dad survived.

Dad dedicated the book to his family's troubled past, and in the introduction he explains why. "The reason I am making my family history available for the public to read is that it is one of the examples of millions of victimized families, people, or persons; an illustration of what the soviet political repression did to them in the beginning of the twentieth century.

"It can be related to by millions who, in the Soviet Union and in Georgia particularly, were destroyed, hurt, resettled, and forced into labor. Their lives were shortened; tens of thousands of people were executed, many of them innocent.

"Yes, it's true that some had outspoken hate against the Communist Party, and it's true that many times this dissatisfaction was exposed and opposed with actions. But there were many who were not forgiven by the 'Cheka,' just because they did not denounce others' oppositional views to their leaders.

"The Cheka was an emergency committee, shortened from Russian words, in which leaders over many years arrested, tortured, and executed thousands of dissidents, deserters, or completely innocent people" (Revaz Kverenchkhiladze, *The Story of the Repressed Family*, Tbilisi, Georgia, 2012).

"Dad, in 1999, when I first arrived in the United States of America, not many understood that the Soviet Union was much more than just Russia. One of the first challenges I faced in America was being identified as a Russian. They did not know how this was a sensitive case for us, due to the long history of conflict amongst Georgians and Russians."

Dad nods in understanding. We talk more, but a telephone ring awakes us into reality.

I have to leave soon.

Suddenly everything shutters around me. Everything freezes. I turn into someone coldhearted and rough-skinned. I have to get tough not to let emotions make me weak. I have to pretend. But deep inside, my trembling heart is crying without sound.

I pick up the phone. "Maka, I am waiting for you by the hallway entrance. It's time to go to the airport," my cousin, Tamara, tells me.

I hug Mom and Dad and kiss them.

"Well, I have to fly now! You know I'll be back soon enough, don't you?" I give some encouraging words, joke, make them smile, then open the door and carry my heavy suitcase outside.

"See you both soon!" My words fly up the stairs as I go down them. Tears bite at my nose before I reach the bottom.

"Let me help you!" With a firm voice, Tamara takes the suitcase.

"See you soon!" I call once more to my parents from the yard.

They both stand on the third-floor balcony, wishing me a safe trip to my new homeland. Sadness radiates from their bodies even though their voices say warm good-byes.

૭

At the airport, my suitcase is checked in.

"Tamara, I have to be strong. What choice do I have?" I try to stop any more tears.

"Maka, you've been so strong always. You overcome so many obstacles?! You inspire us. Don't worry about your parents. We are all here to take care of them. You go be with your boys." Tamara's words have always given me power to go on. Her positive energy is so transforming.

An escalator takes me upstairs, leaving Tamara farther and farther behind. And with her I am leaving part of me there too. Up there at the top of the escalator is a door to fly me to a different world, with different things and thoughts, friends and values, worries and tears.

I go through passport checking. Even though striving for high standards, dressed in dark uniforms, the Georgian security guards have unfriendly, gloomy, serious faces.

In a fraction of a second, my mind recalls arriving at the United States airports. As soon I land and exit the gate, things switch to a joyful and happy mode. I feel free in spirit while passing through that passport control. Oceans of travelers come from all over, but they are all welcome.

On the airplane, I settle into my seat and buckle my seatbelt. Other passengers board, but I avoid eye contact and look out the oval window. Periods of my life start to click through my mind like a slide show. Questions, questions, those challenging questions from friendly and curious Americans start to race in my head:

"Where are you from?" I've been asked this a thousand times.

"I am from Georgia." I've said these words countless times too.

"But you don't have a Southern accent?"

To clarify, I always explain further with a short geographical review and history lesson.

"What brought you here?" is usually the next question, and I answer over and over. Or they phrase it, *"How did you end up in here?"*

For real, how did I end up in America? Where do I belong? What am I doing in this country? Why did I bring my boys there?

The airplane door is shut. The craft backs away from the airport gate in my birth city, and soon rolls forward toward the runway and the open sky.

∅

God knows how many times I've been asked, *"When did you decide to stay in this country?"*

And even today my answer is, *"I have never decided to stay."*

Many times I have made the decision to go back home and never return to America. And yet, every time I fly to Georgia, that same number of times something pulls me back to the United States.

The irony of life is that all experiences and life challenges over time change us. They grow us and give us a whole different perspective on things. So I have continued to change, but amongst all this mess, I am still finding myself out of place.

When years ago I initially flew with my three young boys to America, I fought thousands of doubtful thoughts and emotions. "Four Georgians are leaving their country. The goal is to come back! But who knows where life's paths will lead us, where the invisible ropes will pull us?"

With tears in my eyes now as they were then, I still wish my country hugged me, told me words of comfort, and never let me go from her arms.

There have been a lot of internal, political reasons why Georgians have left their homeland in search of better lives. Emigrants are everywhere, in many different countries, trying to find their places somewhere else. Many of them have survived, or gotten on their feet, and some of them may have even failed. But here we are, sitting in adoptive countries, still wishing for the warm words, care, and love we wished our countries could have given us.

Here we are, still missing our lands each second of our lives, full of sorrow. A mixture of homesickness and nostalgia has become our permanent disease.

A life of prosperity abroad is not a magic bullet for us. Sleepless nights, a constant search for myself, persistently trying to keep the Georgian spirit and talents in my children, endless thoughts about home, family, and friends . . . this is the reality for many of us.

The decisions I made when I was younger, in response to the collapsed country that I lived in, led me to Chicago, the Windy City. At the age of twenty-nine, life tested me and gave me a plethora of problems to solve. My five-year-old son, Levan, who had burnt himself, led us to an unfamiliar world in search of proper treatment. I had a very heavy burden placed on my shoulders with no way out, so I did what I had to. I had to take charge and lead. I became one of the many emigrants, who, during the times of complete uncertainty, went searching for themselves in the foreign lands that gave them shelter and possibilities to survive.

Emigrants are people tested by life, and their fight for survival is both difficult and painful because the soul becomes the main target of all inevitable difficulties.

Countless times I've stood in the Chicago megalopolis and asked myself, "Why did I move out of my country? Why did I leave the place where I had a great childhood, meaningful memories, parents, and friends I could depend on? Why did I come to America? What am I doing here? Where do I belong?"

My inquisitive mind has always strived for some improvements, and in this journey I saw the chance to change my unwanted reality. I read the words of American psychologist James Hillman, "Sooner or later, something seems to call us onto a particular path. . . . This is what I must do, this is what I've got to have. This is who I am."

I realize that this is my road to walk.

☙

After many years of traveling back and forth from one country to another, and changing different houses, I settled in a beautiful, two-story single house with a basement. This might sound confusing to some Americans who are used to nice, big homes, where each member has their own room and privacy, but for me, this new living environment seemed too spacious.

Although my struggles as a single mom raising three boys and my uncertainty as an emigrant were over, I felt lost. Now I was a woman and an emigrant with a status, but ironically, even though it seemed I had everything, still nothing fulfilled my soul.

Soon I realized I never actually found myself.

One hot August day in 2011, I found a book by Parker J. Palmer sitting on my husband's office desk. The title intrigued me with an important message for me saying, *Let Your Life Speak*. I started to read.

My mind, usually busy with many thoughts and unanswered questions, caused me to misread the phrase "finding a vocation" as "finding a vacation."

"Why do we have to find our vacation?" I asked myself a few times, trying to understand what the author meant to say.

As I read further, I was presented with the definition of the word *vocation*. "Vocation, derived from the Latin root for 'voice,' means 'calling that I hear, calling from the heart.'

I felt all my insides tremble, and I heard my inner voice: "Let your life speak!"

At that exact moment, I knew I had to let my life speak. I felt a sense of refreshment, as if someone had given me an ice-cold cup of water in some barren and scorching desert. While I wasn't sure at the time how my life would speak, some inner energy was telling me that I would find the way.

This thought stayed with me and bothered me day and night after reading the book. I could not concentrate on anything, nor were my thoughts clear. I was on the edge knowing that something was going to change.

Then something extraordinary happened, on a sunny September day in 2011. That day I sat on the bleachers and watched my high school senior son, Levan, play soccer, his favorite sport since he was six. I always thought his love of the sport existed because it connected him to his childhood memories in which he lived with his precious grandparents, played with many friends, and spent his first ten years of life.

Although I sat on the bleachers and watched my son play, my thoughts resembled rollercoaster rides going in wild twists and turns. I thought about my own childhood and teenage years, and then the wonderful years that followed at Tbilisi State University, where I earned my degree, a master of language arts of Georgian language and linguistics. My degree was going to waste. Unfortunately, I had never been given a chance to perform with my full potential.

My unclear future plans did not allow me to concentrate on the soccer game. Instead, I stared at the clock for most of the game.

Suddenly, it came to me as fast as a lightning strike, and as clear as the sound of thunder.

"I have to write! I must write down all those thoughts that have been disturbing me all these years, worrying me, and not giving me a break to sleep peacefully!"

In that moment, everything around me made sense. I realized that only writing would soothe my soul.

Subsequently, I remembered the sentence in Parker J. Palmer's book about finding my vocation. "Let your life speak! Tell your story and answer the questions which are bothering you!"

Perhaps my instincts directed me to writing because of my writer dad. All my life I've watched him sitting by his desk with a pen in his hand. The writing environment was very familiar to me—the one full of creative people, book reviews, and poetic events. All that changed after the Soviet Union collapsed, when the years that followed became a time of survival.

My newly found vocation was the answer to bringing that life back. I couldn't wait to write!

Ø

It was December 2011. Usually winters here in Chicago are cold and snowy. But that season definitely spoiled us with warm and dry weather. Matching Christmastime with my maroon-colored coat, I was downtown. Coming here was always a celebration for me, and that day was no exception. Christmas lights and decorations added a dreamy look to the night.

All of us were there—my husband, our four teenage boys, and me. American professional singers from DePaul University of Chicago performed Georgian folk songs in a concert. But the evening's excitement grew because we stayed the night at our friend's condo on the thirty-first floor in a skyscraper. When we entered the condo, my boys ran to the windows.

The condo overlooked roofs of other tall buildings, busy downtown streets, and Lake Michigan. I felt so powerful looking over an entire skyscraper world. Bulletproof windows surrounded us on three sides, creating a feeling of freedom which filled my soul with joy.

I felt so close to the sky.

"Hey, guys, I've found binoculars here!" Sandro announced, and pressed them to his eyes and then to the window. Each of the boys impatiently waited for his turn to look through them.

"Wow, guys, I found chocolate chip cookies!" Now Nika yelled, and the rest of the boys raced there, opening cabinets, searching for more snacks and sweets.

I closed my eyes and became lost in my dreams. In my imagination the condo was mine. I breathed the city life style, I saw myself as an author, I imagined that the next morning I had a meeting with a publisher, then there were presentations, book signings, readers, writers, friends. . . .

✇

Now years have gone by. Mistakes are done. Experiences are gained. Lessons are learned. Values are reevaluated. I have become an author. And I have gone to Georgia many times and then returned.

At first my urge for travel was confusing for Tom. "Why do you have to visit your country for two weeks?"

I tried to explain that these two weeks were not vacations for us emigrants. This was a time to take care of parents, to walk down the streets we grew up playing on and enjoying our worriless childhoods, to breathe the air of friendship, and to fill our souls with memories.

Luckily for me, his attitude toward my frequent travels changed after he visited Georgia, met my people, joined our relationships, tested our traditions, and sampled our foods.

On the way to the airport while leaving the country, he told me, "I'll never ask you again why you want to go back to your homeland."

And after this entire long search for where I belong, the reality is that I live here, in America. I have a family and grown-up children here. This land of freedom has given us shelter and a loving hand. We need to find our place here, something to fulfill us.

And today I tell to my three adult sons, "Since life has brought us here, we should try to use this opportunity to combine experiences and values from both places. This will not only make us stronger, but also may serve for good for others."

In this long search was born the book, which I shared to my people, *A Journey to America*. It is a memoir of my twelve years of experiences learned in this country.

And sharing this book, *A Soul Divided*, with the American reader is part of my nostalgia and part of the search for myself in this new land.

Have I found myself and my place in the universe after all?

During this long journey, unanswered questions finally received answers:

"Where do I belong?"

Now I say, "I belong to both places. Both places fulfill me as a person."

About the Author

Maka Kartheiser (Kverenchkhiladze) was born in 1970 in Tbilisi, the capital city of the country Georgia. She experienced early life in this Soviet Union country and graduated from Tbilisi State University with a BA and MA in Arts of Georgian Language and Literature. In search of improving her life, she started to travel back and forth between the United States and Georgia.

In 2004 she brought her three boys to Chicago and continued working as a nanny and caring for elders to support her children. She built new connections but kept working to preserve the culture, language, and the idea of being "Georgian." Maka sought a state of being where she would fully be able to use her abilities and education. After being a single mom for eight years, she remarried. Combining two cultures and traditions of different families and children has been an experience never to be forgotten.

Living in a small town of Johnsburg, Illinois, raising four young men, and working as a substitute teacher, she shares her knowledge and experiences with the youth of that community.

Maka Kartheiser, cofounder of the Georgian Cultural Center in Chicagoland, was awarded "Successful Emigrant Woman" for her tireless care of Georgian culture, language, and values among emigrants and their families, on March 13, 2017.

A Soul Divided is her fourth book.

Maka published her first memoir, *The Journey to America*, in 2012 in Tbilisi, Georgia, with Universali Publisher;[1] the poem

---

[1] Georgia, Tbilisi, 0179, Ilia Chavchavadze Ave.19. Their e-mail address is universal@internet.ge, and the telephone number is 011 995 2 22 36.

anthology *Soul in Space,* in 2014 in Tbilisi, Georgia, with David Agmashenebeli, Publisher; and *Laptopiada*, a collection of her essays, diaries, and short stories, in 2016 in Tbilisi, Georgia, with Saunje Publishing.[2] All three books are written in the author's native Georgian language.

The Scent of Homeland, a collection of poems from Georgian emigrants from all over the world, includes three poems by Maka Kartheiser. She also originated the idea of creating such a book to showcase emigrants' literary excellence. This is published in the Georgian language by Saunje Publishing.

---

[2] http://saungeo.ge/. Georgia, Tbilisi, 0179, K. Al. Kazbegi St., 32/34. Their e-mail address is saungeo@gmail.com, and the telephone number is 011 995 2 14 12 14.

Made in the USA
Monee, IL
29 May 2023